A Musical Life i
The Royal Marines

John pictured in 1995

The Memoirs of Major John Perkins
ARAM MMus (Dist) LRAM ARCM LGSM Royal Marines

ISBN: 9798651646227

Foreword

My admiration for the Royal Marines Band Service with their fine and versatile music, and invariably immaculate smartness, was born in me when I joined the Royal Navy in 1961; and this admiration went on to grow throughout my 42 years of active service and beyond: it is still as strong now as it has ever been.

There can be no question that the RMBS is without parallel in the world, and it was into this Service that John Perkins dropped in 1965 to spend a fulfilling 35-year career. This volume's account of his life is a marvellous compendium of his work and various activities as musician, violinist, conductor, composer, arranger and recording enthusiast; and, in his later years, as a key figure in the Band's organisation and administration in various Director of Music appointments. Colour is provided as we find laid out for us all the places around the world where he went on duty - many beyond most people's dreams - mainly in the HM Yacht Britannia which he palpably enjoyed to the full; and the story is rich in anecdotes, does not shy away from exposing the occasional down moments, is peppered with the names of his fellow bandsmen over the years (what a memory!) - and the story is told in a light, self-deprecating and entertaining style. This was clearly a man with whom it was fun to be in company, both socially and professionally; and one who made a difference to the benefit of his Service – he was a real force for good. For example, through his playing (especially as a first-class violinist), the changes he pushed through such as degree accreditation for RM musicians, or his recording initiatives - his Ashokan Farewell will be a very special legacy that will be with us for decades to come.

What also comes across is that, underpinned by his adage "Adapt & Overcome", his wholehearted approach to his career gave him ultimate job satisfaction - borne out in the last sentences of the book: "I wish I could turn the clocks back and do it all again!".

This is a most enjoyable read, and I commend it wholeheartedly.

Admiral of the Fleet the Lord Boyce KG GCB OBE DL
Lord Warden of The Cinque Ports

Dedication

These scribblings are dedicated to Cay, Nick, Steve and their families who have been the 'innocent victims' of my service career. Always on the move, and generally without complaint, we have muddled along just fine. Thanks.

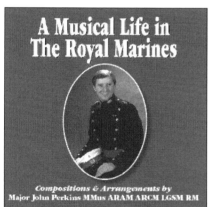

This CD is a recording of some of the compositions and arrangements made by John when serving in The Royal Marines
Cat. No: CLCD16107

This CD is a recording of some of John's orchestral music. Includes Elegy for Strings, Jack's Peace & Cole's Dream
Cat. No: CLCD19912

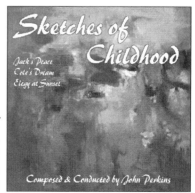

All the recordings mentioned in this book are available to download from iTunes

Contents

ACKNOWLEDGEMENTS

Reference has been made to the following books during research for this book.

The Royal Yacht - Britannia The Official History, Richard Johnstone-Bryden 2003

The Blue Band Magazine - RM Band Service Journal - Volume 41 No 1

A Life on The Ocean Wave - John Trendell

The Memoirs of Major John Perkins
ARAM MMus (Dist) LRAM ARCM LGSM Royal Marines

Preface

Something strange happened three years ago - I retired.

Having spent 66 years as a workaholic I have found free time a challenge, so I have taken to travelling, reading and trying to become a professional golfer! In the course of my life I have been asked many times, "What do you do for a living?" A difficult question, partly because the questioner doesn't really care what you do, but mostly because there is no winning answer. If you really started to tell them all that you do it would sound boastful. If you tell too little you sound suspiciously evasive. If you say, 'a musician' ears prick up and a range of supplementary questions follow to find out exactly what type of musician you might be and any other 'juicy' bits. Almost always the questioner says something like, "I used to play the cello/trumpet" (or something else) then continues to tell you, at some length, how good or bad they were. At this point my eyes glaze over and I regret owning up to music, wishing I had gone for Property Developer, Company Director, Charity Worker or retired Government worker; all the above being true, yet rarely generate supplementary questions.

On those occasions when I have been drawn into explaining some of the details about my life in music, especially my time spent serving in The Royal Yacht Britannia and the many other opportunities that came my way during my 35 years in The Royal Marines (and since I retired in 2000 from the Royal Marines), I am told that I have had an extraordinary life and I should write some of it down.

Because of my reluctance to talk about details of my past, even with family members, I thought it might be of interest to our Grandchildren (3 of the 4 live in Manhattan, New York) to know a little more of their (English) Grandfather, which might explain to them why he is so odd! I have confined myself to the years spent in The Royal Marines which form the first 35 years of my working life. The last twenty years have been equally diverse and challenging, but that is another story.

As best as I can recall, this is my story.

CHAPTER 1

Almost By Accident!

It was Tuesday morning 15th June 1965, a day like many others in my hometown of Deal in Kent, when my schoolboy job was to start the day by cycling to the newsagents to collect my daily delivery of newspapers. I was reminded by the shop owner that Tuesday was the one day each week when we had to deliver magazines and 'glossy' publications in the evening - all good. I was 14 years and 7 months old and, so far, the day was uneventful.

On returning home around 8am my parents informed me that I had to be at the Royal Marines Barracks at 9am to meet with Captain Peter Sumner who was the Director of Music (Training) at the Royal Marines School of Music. I had known Captain Sumner for a year or so because he came each week to conduct the local Deal Youth Orchestra in which I was an aspiring trumpet player. I also knew a little of him because I had for some years been a member of the Royal Marines Volunteer Cadet Force based in the barracks at Deal and he was an occasional visitor. At the time I was the Bandmaster of the Cadet Band, so the Royal Marines Barracks was already a familiar place with my twice weekly attendance for band and cadet training. My father (a former Royal Marine Musician) also worked in the barracks as one of the barbers so I was often in and out with him.

Therefore, with no particular expectations, no money, no possessions (other than my cornet which my father said I would need), I set off on what turned out to be a 35-year adventure. For me, although I didn't realise it at the time, there was no turning back.

1952, John aged 14 months
60 Thornbridge Road, Deal

Having arrived at the Royal Marines School of Music on my bicycle (with my paper-round bag ready for the Tuesday evening deliveries), I met four other boys who had travelled from Portsmouth, Swindon, Dover and Newcastle respectively. Our ages ranged from 14-year-old Timothy Felix Peter Smythe-Rumsby, who measured a mere 4 feet 7 inches, and was by far the shortest man to have joined the Royal Marines, to Vic Clarke at 16 years and a few months. Vic appeared every bit an adult to us young ones, made more so by his size which reflected his pastime as a bodybuilder!

Our reception by the Instructional Staff was formal and we were quickly made to stand in line and told to speak only when spoken to and to start acting like 'Royal Marines', whatever that meant to young school boys! I could see one of our number from Swindon was uncomfortable with this whole procedure. Like us all, he had never really left his hometown before and the nervous tension of the situation was kicking in.

John and sister Mary
1958 at school in Deal

At 10am we were lined up outside the Commanding Officer's Office and one by one marched in to recite our 'attestation' swearing allegiance to the Queen, Her Heirs and Successors for nine years (after the age of eighteen), plus a further three years in the reserves. Wow!

I learned later that my parents must have signed a consent for this to happen, but that was not told to me and I truly believed I would be going off to school after these formalities were over and delivering my 'glossy' magazines sometime later that afternoon. I suppose I thought I was joining the music school as the next step of my Cadet Training which I was already embarked upon. In fact, my new immediate problem was that we were now in basic training for six weeks during which time we could not leave the barracks at any time - how was I going to inform the newsagent? No mobile phones in those days!

Our next stop was the barber's shop for the obligatory short, back and sides, swiftly followed by being marched to the Quartermaster's Store to draw our kit. This kit included everything (but everything) we needed in our daily lives, including a shaving kit - not that any of us had started shaving other than Vic!

I have told this story of my first day to family and friends down the years and sense that those listening assumed I was embellishing the facts to make for a good story, but that is not the case. Those who travelled from afar to begin their career may have had a more traumatic experience than me and some, including our fellow new entrant from Swindon, couldn't cope at all and were let go back to their parents when it became obvious they were not suited to life in the Royal Marines. I had grown up in and around the Royal Marines barracks at Deal and been a Royal Marines Cadet, so the transition for me was easier to deal with, although I did quickly realise this was not a temporary situation and I needed to make the best of things. Besides, I didn't enjoy the learning process in school other than music and French at which I shone. The prospect of leaving school was just fine as far as I was concerned.

It was a very different time in the mid 1960s and we were just a few of many hundreds of boys (girls became part of our number in 1992) who joined the Royal Marines School of Music under these circumstances. It was the only branch of the Armed Forces that you could join aged 14 years - quite an attraction for poor achievers at school such as I. This was also a time when there were few ways of achieving a discharge from the services. It would be some considerable number of years before buying your discharge became a possibility so, short of medical or disciplinary reasons, we were in for a while!

For most of us it was the best thing we could have ever done and changed our lives for the better in every way. Not that we knew it then.

Class 4A South Deal School 1961-62
John 3rd Row - 5th from left

CHAPTER 2

A Musical Family

I was born on 28th November 1950 one of five children, two older sisters (Eileen and Margaret) and two younger sisters (Mary and Christine). Being the only boy afforded me certain benefits, in my father's eyes, as it was our (the children's) collective belief that father did not care for girls as much as boys and was not always as kind as he should have been to them. He had a short fuse and was given to outbursts of temper with little provocation, often resulting in some form of violence. Nothing extreme, but enough to establish a permanent atmosphere of tension in the house once Dad was home.

In fairness to him, he had joined the Royal Marines Band Service himself in 1938 just prior to the outbreak of WW2 and served throughout the war in ships seeing many terrible things and living in constant danger. Today, Post-Traumatic Stress Disorder is commonly diagnosed and treated, as opposed to the 'coverall' at the time 'shell-shocked' which applied to so many returning servicemen and women. He received no medical treatment that I am aware of and continued to serve in the Royal Marines until 1958 when he retired to Deal, my mother's home town. Those who served with my father will recall him as one of the great characters of the Band Service, known more for his exploits, such as running tea boats, cutting hair, making and selling horseradish sauce and working other less formal rackets, rather than his cornet playing. He was nevertheless a natural musician with a very good ear for music and could busk pretty much any tune to order. Dad's harmless military escapades occasionally found him getting into hot water. He wrote down one such example for me to include in the Blue Band Magazine when I was The Editor in 1990.

My parents John & Joyce Perkins' wedding day 8th May 1943
Back, L to R: Grandad and Granny Perkins, Uncle Bill, SA Officer, Grandad Bird
Front, L to R: Auntie Dorrie, John & Joyce Perkins, Granny Bird

10

'Wrong Patient'

In 1944, I was a one-badge musician serving with the Royal Marines in Deal, Kent. I had been married about 12 months and my wife was expecting her first child. During early pregnancy she was frequently ill with the usual symptoms.

One morning when she was really bad I decided to remain at home with her sending word to the Barracks that I was sick and to excuse my absence from duty that day. About two hours later an ambulance arrived at my house with a naval doctor and a male nurse seeking a prospective patient. My wife noticed the ambulance from her bedroom window and shouted down to me the unhappy news. There was I, halfway through scrubbing the floor, sweating drops of ink and not in a fit state to receive visitors. From then on it was panic stations and action stations as my wife and I immediately changed roles. She jumped out of bed and I jumped in just having enough sense to put my pyjamas on. After letting the doctor in and telling him where the patient was, my wife remained silent, and downstairs.

Well, when the doctor examined me, he noticed that I was perspiring profusely and my heartbeat was at a fast tempo, so he decided to have me in the infirmary for treatment and told me to get dressed and get in the ambulance and I was carted off to the Barracks, staying there for five days with constant care and attention, not daring to let on that there was nothing wrong with me and that it was my wife who was ill and not me!'

My mother and father met in Deal in 1942 and married at the Salvation Army (SA) Citadel on the 8th May 1943. This proved eventful and was a microcosm of the two sides of the family. My mother, the lone child growing up quietly within the church environment and my father one of a large family of nine children from the Erith/Belvedere area of South London to a merchant seaman father (who played the concertina very well by ear) and his Irish (allegedly wild and unpredictable) wife. All the children were musical to various degrees and one sister, who died in her twenties, was a particularly gifted pianist we were told. On the wedding day my father's family travelled by train from London to Deal arriving around lunchtime for the wedding which was to be held in the SA Citadel at 3pm that day. With two hours to spare it was decided to repair to the nearest pub where my Irish Grandmother downed four pints of Guinness in quick time, something which was well rehearsed in her case! The wedding time approached and visiting Grandmother presented at the SA Citadel (a teetotal environment) singing all her favourite songs along the route and gathering vocal support from passing strangers as was the norm in 1943 war-torn Britain. Needless to say this was received with shock and horror by my Mother's family as well as the SA 'great and good' who were presiding. The least said about the reception that followed the wedding the better, but the day is part of our family folklore that improves with each subsequent telling!

My mother grew up as a member of the Salvation Army Church of which she remained a lifelong member. In fact we all attended the SA, most of us in SA uniform, even my father, a heavy smoker and frequent drinker attended. I think for us children the big attraction was the music, both singing and playing in the band.

I started learning to play the cornet at the age of seven and became a member of the SA Junior Band shortly afterwards. The SA has produced many fine musicians down the years who have gone on to become leading players in Brass Bands, Orchestras, Military Bands and any variation on the above. I was always attracted to the more emotive music which the SA specialises in. Composers such as Eric Ball and Sir Dean Goffin typified this in pieces such as 'Kingdom Triumphant' and 'The Light of the World'. Once heard they remain with you for life.

John (left) 1962 aged 11 years outside the SA Citadel West Street Deal with David English

We were all members of the Deal Corps where, coincidentally, a Bandmaster Dockrill had retired to a few years earlier. Bandmaster Dockrill was a published composer and arranger and impressive all-round musician who, after some persuading by my father, agreed to take me on as a student of theory of music and basic composition when I was about 11 years old. I think I was a bit star-struck in the lessons and I am unsure what exactly I achieved, but I do remember starting to believe that maybe music was the life for me.

Life growing up in the mining community of Deal was fairly austere, certainly by today's standards. Post-war rationing remained in place until 1954 and televisions and modern-day electrical appliances had yet to find their way into the average home. Other than the Bible and the Salvation Army Hymnal I doubt we had a book in the house. Besides music, there was no concept of home learning. Career expectations for us children were low. Happily, over time, this expectation was proved wrong.

I remember arriving at school one day to be told we were going to sit the 11-plus examination. Papers were put in front of us and I floundered for the next few hours trying to make sense of the questions, which were quite unlike anything I had seen previously, either at school or at home. Needless to say, I failed!

I enjoyed rugby at school (we didn't play football or cricket) and woodwork was another favourite subject, although I showed no particular talent as a carpenter. Most of the teachers in this post-war period were elderly and they appeared short-tempered and easily riled (no doubt years of wartime being a major factor), which in turn led to corporal punishments being a daily occurrence. The cane, the slipper and the ruler were the weapons of choice and I suppose we became used to them. Our French teacher, who shall remain nameless, had the habit of throwing the chalkboard rubber at any child misbehaving. Thankfully this is all inconceivable today. I'd like to say it did us no harm, but I am certain it did us no good either!

At around 9 years old I joined the local colliery band, 'Betteshanger Colliery Brass Band' in the junior section. It was my good fortune to be amongst some very proficient brass players who had settled in Deal, partly because they had found work in the Kent Coalfield which had five pits and, more importantly two bands. Deal was also the home of the Royal Marines School of Music which could boast expert players both in the resident Staff Band and on the Instructional Staff at the music school. On the teaching staff was Professor Walter Hargreaves, the renowned teacher of cornet/trumpet and multi-award-winning conductor of the top brass bands in the country. On joining the Royal Marines Band Service some years later I went on to study the cornet/trumpet with Walter Hargreaves for three years.

Members of the Salvation Army Deal, Junior Band
John centre

My weekly routine at this time was Music Theory lessons Mondays, SA band practice Tuesday, Betteshanger band practice Wednesday, Royal Marines Cadets Thursday, concerts at the weekend with both bands interspersed with church services/Sunday school, all of which included music making of some form. So it was no surprise that at the age of 13 years I joined the Deal Youth Orchestra under the direction of Captain Peter Sumner, which in turn led me towards joining the Royal Marines a year later (without audition as Captain Sumner knew me well enough by this time) at 14 years and 7 months as a cornet/trumpet player, quite a good player I might add, although doubtless some may disagree!

CHAPTER 3

The Royal Marines School of Music

It was the task of the RMSM to produce musicians who were able to play two or more instruments so they could perform in the Military Concert Band, the Orchestra, the Dance Band and other musical combinations within these broad mediums. This was a requirement of the Naval Service and written into Royal Marines Instructions. There were two main exceptions to this rule which were those of 'Solo Cornet' and 'Solo Clarinet' as both of these categories could play in bands and orchestras. There were a limited number of people in these 'solo' categories and in practice most clarinettists also learned to play the saxophone.

The RMSM was organised in its current form by Lt Col Sir Vivian Dunn (the first Military Musician to be Knighted in 1969), who was appointed Principal Director of Music for the Naval Service (The Royal Marines being part of the Royal Navy) in 1953. The School was to be based in the historic Napoleonic barracks at Deal in Kent, which would also combine new entry training for 'Commando' Royal Marines as well as specialist training for Drivers, Physical Training Instructors, Drill Instructors and others. It would also encompass career advancement training for musicians up to Warrant Officer Bandmaster level. The barracks at Deal was a vibrant place in the 1960s with up to 2000 serving personnel plus civilian staff and dependent families living in the community.

New Entry Training

In 1965 The Royal Marines School of Music gave young 14-year-olds the opportunity to learn music at one of the leading music institutions in the country - and so much more. All this was to reveal itself to me over the next 3 years as the system assesses where you are, identifies what you need and encourages those who wish to succeed (that was definitely me). As a bonus, it also allowed me to leave school and focus on a subject in which I had some talent, and be paid for it (albeit only '30 Bob' each week - £1.50 in decimal currency). So my - almost accidental - entry as described earlier was the first of many lucky coincidences that happened to me over the years.

The Royal Marines School of Music was, arguably, the most complete and well-rounded of all music colleges, the basic instrumental course being between 3 - 4 years long depending on the age of entry. The Initial New Entry course was six weeks long and was the basic indoctrination into service life, teaching life skills such as laundry, ironing, personal hygiene, time management as well as the more obvious subjects of drill, swimming[1], Corps History and all things Royal Marines. There was no music taught during this process and the New Entrants were mostly kept apart from other trainees for the duration. All this was under the guidance of a Drill Instructor, who became our surrogate Mother/Father/Teacher/Mentor. Our Drill Instructor was a terrific man named Corporal Sam Mclachlan (RIP Sam) who seemed so old and experienced (and military!) to us, when in reality he was only in his mid-twenties. Sam was everything I imagined a Drill Instructor might be (based on black and white Ealing movies I had seen about National Service current in those days) and he both terrified us and protected us in equal measure. Years later, I met Sam when I was undertaking my Special Duties Officers' Course at the Commando Training Centre, Lympstone (1984) as a Warrant Officer First Class (Bandmaster), prior to Commission to Lieutenant Director of Music. Sam couldn't have been prouder of 'one of his boys' making so much progress through the ranks. It confirmed my earlier thoughts as to what a nice man he was. Sam was long retired from active service at this point, but had a civilian job in the stores.

At the end of the 6-week New Entry course just four of the initial five who started remained, with our friend from Swindon having parted company as unsuitable for service life. The 'Best Boys Plaque' went to Timothy Felix Peter Smythe-Rumsby who had become a minor celebrity being the shortest man to ever join the Royal Marines, who coincidently also had the longest name to have joined The Corps. Unfair advantages I say!

After a long weekend to visit families for the first time in six weeks it was onto music training.

Passing Out parade August 1965 - John far right
Spot the 'best boy' in the middle!

[1] It was mandatory for Royal Marines to be able to swim. Not so for sailors for whom it was optional. A sink or swim policy tended to do the trick!

Music Training

Without warning, another unexpected turn of events happened on the day we returned from our long weekend. We assembled at the Supply Officer Music's Department to be issued with our musical instruments as designated from the audition process. I learned some time later that it was common to recruit young men who showed musical promise even if there was no vacancy on the instrument they played, such was the pressure on recruiting the high numbers required. On joining they would simply be issued with a different instrument in a shortage category which they then had to learn from scratch! I turned out to be a variation on this theme as there was a shortage of violinists in the School, so as well as being issued with a cornet and trumpet I was given a rather battered violin with the instruction that my musical category was now 'Cornet & Violin'. I complained, but to no avail, and, having learned from my New Entry Training that to argue was not a good idea, I walked away with an instrument which was to define the rest of my career both in the Royal Marines and subsequently civilian life. What luck!

Another change took place in The RMSM shortly after this time with the appointment of a new Director of Music Training Captain Paul Neville, a wonderful man and musician who became Principal Director of Music in 1968 replacing Lt Col Sir Vivian Dunn. Paul was a breath of fresh air and, although he always kept himself at arm's length, he was quick to encourage interested musicians and brought an enthusiasm to whatever he was involved with. He soon established a boys' choir which became very good and was part of concert presentations throughout training. This helped with aural training and was fun. I served with Paul as the Leader of his Staff Orchestra in the mid 1970s and took over as conductor of the Kent Concert Orchestra when he retired from music altogether in 2007. Paul and his wife Anne were always perfectly charming to me and, from a musical viewpoint, my time spent with Paul in the late 1970s was the most influential of my career.

I was lucky to have been born with a very good aural sense which is a massive bonus as both a violinist and especially a conductor. I also had a very good memory for music and I could remember the broad brush of the page of music with only a glance when conducting. A good aural sense is so important when conducting (and playing of course) and a certain amount can be taught to improve, but it seems to me it is something you either have naturally or not.

CHAPTER 4

The Cornet

M usic training was separated geographically by instrumental category, so all the cornet & violins would practice and be taught in certain rooms as would all the other music categories. My Professor of cornet was Walter Hargreaves who I had known for a number of years through the local Betteshangar Brass Band where Walter was the guest conductor for musical contests around the country. Walter was somewhat of a legend in the Brass Band world and had recently been the winning conductor of the National Championships in the Royal Albert Hall. He was a very short (less than 5 feet tall) Scotsman who could be quite ruthless as a conductor. He was affectionally known as the 'wee professor' because of his stature, but he had a presence when in rehearsal that kept the players riveted to his every word. As a teacher he was very encouraging and I looked forward to lessons with him.

I think overall that I was somewhat of a disappointment to Walter as I didn't really make the rapid progress as a cornet player that was expected of me. My basic problem was that I was taught poorly when I started years earlier and I could not 'unlearn' these bad habits to adopt the modern 'non-pressure' methods that were more successful. The other factor was that I was suddenly part of a wider group of cornet players from all over the British Isles some of whom were superb players already, none more so than someone who became a lifelong friend Alan Upton. Alan had been the National Brass Band Solo Junior Champion at the age of 13 and played in the famous Desford Colliery Band with the likes of Jimmy Watson (later top orchestral Principal Trumpet and Professor of Trumpet at The Royal Academy of Music). Others such as Jon Yates, Dick Grainger, Jeff Miller, Bill Sabine (RIP), 'Haggis' Graydon and Bill Robinson were all in various stages of training during this time. There were many others too who became very good players.

Previously at school I had always been the exceptional musician, but now I found myself as a much smaller fish in this larger pool, a new experience which started to bring out the competitive side of my nature. I continued playing the cornet until 1980 when I was promoted Warrant Officer Bandmaster which meant I no longer played in the band. Now, all these years later, I wish I had kept it going if only as a hobby. Other musicians are probably relieved that I gave it up!

The Violin

The story of the violin could not be more different as within two years I progressed from not playing the instrument at all to passing Grade 8 with Distinction at a hastily arranged exam held in the Royal College of Music. The exam in London was arranged by Lt Col Sir Vivian Dunn because the normal exam dates conflicted with a musical tour of Yorkshire by the Training Band. Vivian Dunn had this type of reach in all areas of the music profession at the time, stemming from his time as a student at the Royal Academy of Music and subsequent position as one of the original violins in the BBC Symphony Orchestra when formed in 1930.

I had known Lt Col F Vivian Dunn (known as 'Fred' within the Band Service or sometimes 'God' as his birthday was 25th December!) since childhood as my father was for a long time in his band and acted in his service in other ways. Making horseradish sauce which Fred was partial to and in later years acting as the caretaker for the concert hall and sometimes cutting his hair were just some of his sidelines. It was on these occasions that I first got to be in contact with him. He was still Principal Director of Music throughout my training and when I moved to Portsmouth I led the orchestra for his final series of concerts in which I remember playing Mozart's 2nd Violin Concerto in D. As an aside, Sir Vivian used to keep an eye on our two sons, Nick and Steve, when they were in school at Ardingly College near Haywards Heath. Sir Vivian (then long retired) lived just three miles away and often took them for Sunday lunch, terrifying them with his terrible driving and chain smoking throughout the whole time. Not the popular image of the great man!

During the 1960s there was a requirement to train high numbers of violinists at the School, to which end there were four professors of violin - Frank Whitford, Mr Jocelyn, Lew Becker and Harry Lipman. The least successful of these was Harry Lipman whose impatience was legendary and his interpersonal skills basically non-existent. It was just his way. Harry was a fine violinist having been taught at the Royal Northern College of Music by Brodsky himself. He had all the tricks and could play by memory on request most all of the repertoire with an accompanying story or two! He chain smoked and took snuff, possibly the grossest of all habits. He was a one-time member of the London Philharmonic Orchestra and spent 20 years as Leader of the Worthing Symphony Orchestra in the days when seaside orchestras numbered some 20 professional players and were the popular entertainment throughout the summer seasons. In truth Harry was not cut out for teaching and most boys dreaded his lessons. Most famously Jon Yates, the legendary trumpet player, whose brief time as a violinist was spent with Harry until Harry 'tapped' Jon's elbow one time too many and Jon sent him flying across the room! Jon's punishment was to be taken off the violin to become a 'solo cornet' player - the rest is history - sweet deal!

1966 playing football in the old cemetery North Barracks
L to R: Oscar Peterson, Alan Upton, John Perkins, Dickie Valentine

Like Jon Yates, I too was a reluctant violinist at first, but for some reason Harry fascinated me with his playing and his persona and I began to like the sound the violin made once I could make some sense of it. I remember sitting in the Junior Orchestra for the first time after about six months learning the violin. This initial sensation of sitting in the middle of a string section I remember to this day, albeit the orchestra was low standard made up mostly of beginners and we were playing 'Forgotten Dreams' by Leroy Anderson - hardly the most inspiring of pieces. This was a turning point.

Once I had reached this point I became an obsessive practicer and took every opportunity to get extra lessons with Harry. This was easier than it sounds as many of the boys found any excuse to miss his lessons! After a while Harry used to come and find me if another boy didn't turn up, I even went to his bedsit accommodation to practice for civilian concerts (mostly choral concerts) he had asked me to join him for, or for Grade exams which I went through rapidly. It seemed that progress came painfully slowly to me with the cornet above a certain level, but came very naturally to me with the violin. It is fair to point out that at that time the general standard of string playing was poor as opposed to brass and woodwind which was high. So anyone who was a reasonable string player stood out. There were a few of us interested in learning to play string instruments so we formed a string quartet together and had the idea of auditioning for 'Opportunity Knocks' with the legendary Hughie Green. Needless to say our enthusiasm for this was quickly extinguished by our instructors who thought us quite mad. My fellow quartet members were (I think) 'Dusty' Miller (violin), Bill Callow (Viola) and Mick Sole (Cello).

The Cassel Prize

The big annual Solo performance competition in the Music School was The Cassel Prize, endowed by Sir Felix Cassel. A silver medal and a bronze medal were awarded annually to the Royal Marines School of Music, the Royal Military School of Music (Kneller Hall) and the Royal Air Force School of Music.

Other internal prizes were awarded annually for each instrumental category and for aural, but the Cassel Prize was the big one. We were entered into the competition by our music professors if we were thought to be of the necessary standard. At least two qualifying rounds took place to identify the eight remaining players who would compete in the Cassel Prize final which was held in front of an audience and presided over by The Principal Director of Music (Lt Col Vivian Dunn during my time). This was a great way to make your mark on the music scene within the wider Band Service. I was in the 1968 Final as the only violinist and eventually came out as the Runner-Up to 'Dusty' Miller the Saxophone player (I was robbed!).

The Cassel Prize Final 1968
Back L to R: John Beddow, Dave Lambert, Charlie Fleming
Middle: Graham Verroken, Pete Rose, Alan Upton, Brian Key, Bob Metcalf
Front: Capt. Leo Arnold, 'Dusty' Miller, Sir Vivian Dunn, John Perkins, Capt. Peter Sumner

Apart from travelling to the Worshipful Company of Musicians in London to collect our medals we were also asked to play our solo items with the Staff Orchestra at one of the regular orchestral Winter Concerts. A further 'outing' was to an audience of former RM Musicians and Buglers at the annual Band Service Reunion held in Eastney Barracks Portsmouth - pressure gig!

The concert held in Deal with the Staff Orchestra proved to be another one of those lucky twists of fate that changed everything for me yet again. In the audience was The Director of Music of The Royal Yacht Band (Captain Tom Lambert) who was visiting Deal for a meeting. Quite coincidentally he was also desperate to find a violinist at short notice to take over from his current Leader (which requires playing solos that most players try to avoid!) of the Orchestra in the Royal Yacht who had just been sacked for some cardinal sin or other. I was called forward to meet with Captain Lambert the morning after the concert when he informed me that, on the basis of what he had heard in the concert the night before, I was to join him as Leader of the Orchestra in Portsmouth in early September, and be prepared to sail on 14th October 1968 in HMY Britannia for a Royal visit to Brazil! Again, quite by chance, my life was redirected to become one of the elite band of 26 Musicians and buglers that lived and travelled with the Royal Family all over the world, a position I held for a little over seven years!

But, before moving on to life in Britannia, there is a big and equally important aspect of being part of the Royal Marines School of Music.

Music isn't everything!

CHAPTER 5

Junior Wing Life

The collective name for the various Houses that became home to all us boys was Junior Wing. Gloucester House (green flashes) and Neptune House (red flashes) were the group houses for Junior Musicians and Barham House (light blue flashes) was the house for Junior Buglers. Junior Wing was housed in the North end of the New Intake block (now demolished for housing) with Junior Marines and Recruits (both Commando New Entrants) housed in the Southern end. The Commando Junior Marines new entrants were a minimum of 16 years 6 months and the Recruits were considered as adults of at least 17 years 6 months. Junior Musicians and Buglers were like younger children and rarely did the two groups mix. In 1972 all Commando new entrants moved to the newly named 'Commando Training Centre' at Lympstone Devon and the purpose of the barracks at Deal became solely for music training.

I was put into Gloucester House (a little like the Harry Potter 'sorting hat' sequence!) under the watchful eye of CSgt 'Dinger' Bell, an older Commando branch Royal Marine who was our father figure and Headmaster rolled into one. Dinger was terrific with us boisterous teenagers and served in that position for many years.

Each room housed six Junior Musicians and was commanded by a 'boy' Non-Commissioned Officer (NCO) who was called a 'Section Commander'. Above Section Commander was a 'Diamond' and top of the leadership structure was the 'House Captain' or 'No 1 Diamond'. It was thus that the chain of command idea, that is the bedrock of the discipline in the Armed Forces, was first introduced to us.

At any one time there were a hundred or more boys aged between 14 and 18 years of age living and working together 24 hours each day. Most boys soon found others who might have similar interests to them so tended to form groups within the group. My early friends tended to be close to my age and included Peter Rutterford (who like me became a Director of Music in later life), Andy Clarkson (who didn't!) and fellow brass band enthusiasts Alan Upton, Trevor Attwood and Bill Robinson who became regulars with my old Betteshanger Brass Band. Over the next three years we attended the Sunday morning brass band practice then all went back to my parents' house where my mother would treat us all to Sunday lunch (followed often by Cherry Pie - wow!), a rare luxury away from galley meals.

It came as a slight shock to me, having been such a poor student at school before joining, that all boys under the age of 16 years were expected to attend schooling lessons in a range of subjects. Looking back I expect this was a legal requirement, so part of the Infirmary Barracks

1/67 SECTION COMMANDERS COURSE
Commenced Course 15-2-67

DEPOT ROYAL MARINES, DEAL
Completed Course 22-2-67

Barker, J.   Cox, B. A.   Atkinson, R. P.   Rumming, D. W.
Bagnall, R.   Pickering, A. J.   Miller, A. R.   Westwell, J.   Beddow, J. T.   Perkins, J.   Hollingworth, R. A.
Lt. C. Hickinbotham, R.M.   Major R. A. Campbell, R.M.   Sgt. G. Bartlett
(Course Officer)   (O.C. 'J' Wing)   (Course Instructor)

Section Commanders' Course 1/67

(long since demolished for housing) was designated as 'The School'. Lessons included English and Maths and the educational qualifications were NAMET exams which, unfortunately, counted for nothing in the civilian world. At some point towards the end of my training six of us boys were given classroom lessons in music with the aim of undertaking GCE Music. I think we all passed, so my only meaningful qualification aged 17 was GCE Music (O Level).

Alongside all the above there were leadership advancement courses which lasted a week or so and mainly centred around drill and marching type tasks, including voice projection and power of command and other leadership challenges to solve; much like the civilian world has adopted in recent years for management training. From this the 'Section Commanders' and 'Diamonds' were identified and the promotion ladder was refreshed as older boys left training.

Another weekly ritual was Church Parade on Sunday mornings. All boys had to attend this parade and then be marched to church to attend the 11am service. Some boys sang in the choir, otherwise you sat as a group in the barracks church of St Michael and All Angels[2]. However, there were two other alternatives. One was to attend the non-denominational service which was conducted in a secular building by a member of staff and the other was to attend the Salvation Army Citadel which was based in the town centre of Deal. For many, including me as a life-long Salvationist, this was the preferred option as we avoided Church Parade and met as a group (often 20 or more of us) and marched in uniform through the streets of Deal (there being so much less traffic in the 1960s) until we reached the Salvation Army where we were dismissed to go inside. At this point the opportunity for deception was too tempting and many of us would disperse into the town for some adventure, or, in my case, hurry with my friends to the other end of town to attend the rehearsal of the brass band followed by lunch with Mum. As far as I am aware our ruse was never discovered, although looking back I am sure a blind eye was turned to the whole escapade.

Sport was very much part of life and we attended PT lessons twice each week. Wednesday afternoons were given over to team sports when we all piled into buses to travel to the RM sports fields at Coldblow, just outside the town of Deal. Cold, wet and windy is my lasting memory of these times, although I am sure we had fun. PT was a different thing and ranged from the traditional rope climbing and vaulting to boxing, not the best activity for musicians, yet the Band Service has produced a number of talented boxers down the years. I have always been a big fan of fitness training and played sports all my life, especially racket sports and golf.

Musicians are generally good at games and bands can always field a football or rugby side and regularly come out winners against other branches of the services. However, the obsession with running as the only test of fitness has curtailed many a career, wrongly in my view, and continues to blight the occasional very talented musician even today.

Another activity in the non-musical area to take place each year was adventure training, which in my time took place over two weeks in the North-West of Scotland at a place called Loch Ewe. We would set off in uniform for the marathon journey by train, as far as the line would take us, then transfer to 4-ton trucks to take us the remaining distance to the remote loch-side camp which was to be home for the next two weeks. To make sure we got full value out of this trip it always took place in winter when Scotland was at its most challenging!

John - Spring 1968
No 1 Diamond and House
Captain of Gloucester House

---

[2] I was Christened in St Michael and All Angels Church as were our two sons Nicholas and Stephen 28 years later.

Each day started with a dip in the loch followed by daily exercises (PT) and breakfast before moving on to the main activity of the day. This took the form of map marching or hill climbing (big hills!) and screeing down the side of the hill to descend. It was fun I must say, albeit similar to the script of the film 'The Dirty Dozen', but we survived and these trips became the stuff of reunion type tales for years to come.

In the fullness of time I too became a Section Commander, No 1 Diamond and House Captain. I confess that I liked being in charge even at this early stage. On leaving training I was presented with The Commandant General's Certificate for the most promising leadership student.

Loch Ewe outward bound training 1967
John second from right

CHAPTER 6

Eastney Barracks & The Portsmouth Band

On 9th September 1968 I travelled to Portsmouth with two trombone players who were leaving training with me to join their first band - 'The Band of HM Royal Marines Portsmouth'. They were Dally Atkinson (RIP)[3], who became a member of the 'James Shepherd Versatile Brass' some years later before emigrating to Australia, and Charlie Fleming. Charlie has been a life-long friend and we served in the Royal Yacht together for a number of years. In 1992, when I joined The Commandos Band as the Director of Music, Charlie and Ken Schooley, another ex-Yachty, were in the band. Charlie and Ken had left the Royal Marines aged 40, only to rejoin again, just prior to my arrival, for a further five years. It was terrific to see them again and pick up where we left off 20 years earlier.

In the 1960s we travelled on Draft in uniform[4] with our kit bags, musical instruments and anything else we could carry. Deal to Portsmouth via London took most of the day. On arrival we were met by Band Colour Sergeant Graham Hoskins in a Military Vehicle who welcomed us to Portsmouth and managed to squeeze us, and all our kit into the back. Years later, in 1982, Graham was appointed Principal Director of Music in the rank of Lieutenant Colonel when we were to serve together once again, this time in Deal.

The Portsmouth Band was based in Eastney Barracks at that time and was the large band from which 26 of its number were selected each year to serve in HMY Britannia. In practice the same personnel stayed in the Yacht Band unless there was a compelling reason for them to move. If this happened a replacement would be drawn from the wider Portsmouth Band. I had the good fortune to be involved in all the Royal Tours between 1968 and 1975 when I left the band to undertake the 1-year Bandmasters' Course at the RMSM Deal.

Life in Eastney Barracks was very different from what I had been used to in training at Deal. For the first time I had complete freedom to go and do what I wanted when not at work. We lived in long dormitories with as many as ten people to a room, all of whom, it seemed to us, were old hands and colourful characters. I doubt the oldest was more than 25 years old, but so

---

[3] Dally had webbed toes. The only time I have ever seen this in a human. He became a very fine water polo player - seriously!

[4] It was the norm to wear uniform to and fro work, moving from one establishment to another and frequently for 'runs ashore'. Garrison towns such as Portsmouth and Plymouth were always filled with sailors and marines in uniform. Not until the 'troubles' in Northern Island made their way to the mainland did this change when it became forbidden to wear uniform outside of the barracks.

different to us 'newbies'. Rehearsals took place in the morning after any parade or 'Divisions'[5] had finished. The Director of Music was Captain Tom Lambert, a flamboyant man who always appeared to me to be conducting in a mirror, being so concerned as to how he looked! He was very aloof from us musicians and enjoyed being 'an officer' and all that went with it. He was a strong musician which I respected, and there was always a healthy tension in the band when he was conducting. The standards seemed very high to me and I remember thinking I am going to have to work to make my mark in this band. I could never forgive Tom Lambert for giving me the embarrassing job of washing his underwear on my first yacht trip. This required me to hang his 'smalls' (which were not small, but service issue pants!) in the Junior Rates drying room, a cause of much hilarity with others onboard. An early lesson for me in how 'not to do things' as a boss.

After the morning rehearsal all the single men normally went for lunch in the galley which was rapidly followed by a change to civilian clothes and adjournment to the pub outside the main gate, The Eastney Cellars, known to us all as 'Ma Rines' (pronounced as 'Ma Rings' for some reason). 'Ma Rines' was the cultural hub of the band and all significant occasions were celebrated there from birthdays to funerals. The speed at which beer was consumed was intimidating for us 17-year-olds, although we tried our best to keep up with the big boys. Needless to say this did not end well.

Two other early impressions remain with me, the first was the high number of people who smoked, and the second was the musicians obsession with Indian food, which hitherto had passed me by. We smoked everywhere in those days, from cinemas to aircraft, and the exception was the non-smoker. Thankfully this is now totally reversed as education as to the health risks are known to all. As for Indian food, the draw is stronger than ever!

Rum, Baccy and a bit of the 'other'

Many in the Portsmouth Band at that time were seasoned professionals in the art of socialising, having spent years at sea or in Naval establishments when the daily tot of rum was served to all at Midday. The rum ration (commonly called 'tot') was a daily amount of rum given to sailors on Royal Navy ships. It was abolished on 31st July 1970 after concerns that regular intakes of alcohol would lead to unsteady hands when working machinery. It consisted of one-eighth of an imperial pint (71ml) of rum at 95.5 proof, given out to every sailor daily. Sailors (and Royal Marines when serving with the Navy) under 20 years of age were not permitted a rum ration, and were marked on the ship's books as 'UA' (Under Age). This UA status applied to me for my whole time in Britannia as my 20th birthday was not until 28th November 1970. The daily 'tot' was then replaced by three small cans of beer, lager or cider per man, per day; but they had to

---

[5] The Naval equivalent to a parade.

be paid for, albeit Duty-Free. When women were allowed to serve on HM Ships, the choice of booze expanded to include cans of wine. Both sexes could choose two cans of wine per person per day, each can the equivalent to a glass of wine.

'Blue-Liners'. Boy, how we all seemed to smoke! Navy-Cut cigarettes differed from normal fags, in that they were more tightly packed with baccy, therefore stronger. People who smoked them said that 'they were very seriously strong'. Also, Navy cigarettes were duty free. To prevent smuggling and selling on at a profit, they had a blue line along the length in unfiltered, and ending before the filter in others. They were known as 'Blue-liners'.

For many it was a sad day when on the 27th January 1989 'Blue-Liners' were withdrawn, nearly twenty years after the Rum ration had ceased. Blue-Liners were issued to sailors serving in Shore Establishments. For those serving afloat, the packaging was endorsed with 'H.M. Ships Only' and this endorsement was added to each and every cigarette along its length. Many in the navy smoked Blue-Liners so they were considered a much-treasured perk.

In today's changed world, it is worth recalling that the term 'homosexual' (the term 'Gay' was not commonly used at the time) was known to all us boys under training and was generally accompanied by some childish sniggering. This was mostly because for the vast majority of us it was an area of great mystery, to say nothing of being illegal in the Armed Forces at that time. Every now and again rumours would abound that two boys had been caught up to 'no good' and they would mysteriously disappear as if by magic - discharged! It was rare, but it did happen at least a couple of times during my training. Imagine our surprise when we arrived in Royal Marines Barracks Eastney to join the Portsmouth Band to find an overt culture of homosexuality existing from within our number and with little or no attempt at concealment. Yes, it was still illegal to be a practicing homosexual until 32 years later! Gay and lesbian citizens have only been allowed to serve openly in Her Majesty's Armed Forces since 2000.

I remember coming back from watching Derby play Chelsea at Stamford Bridge one Saturday with Charlie Fleming (a lifelong Derby supporter - poor thing!) to hear unexpected noises coming from the two adjoining bathrooms just outside our dormitory. Having only been in the band for a couple of weeks we were a bit green to life in the quiet hours. Our initial thoughts were that someone might be drunk and in difficulties in the bath, so we went to investigate. Finding the bathroom door locked we went to the next bathroom which only had a three quarters wall in between the two baths, so we stood on the empty bath and looked over. What we saw[6] cannot be unseen, and caused many a sleepless night for me and Charlie over the next few weeks. Up to this point I don't think either of us had much of a clue about the homosexual world, but we soon got the message.

---

[6] Was one of the band members and a sailor from Britannia. They were living as a couple at the time.

Not that anyone was 'interested' in us personally, in fact life could not have been more convivial. A great bunch of lads who were always up for a 'run-ashore', invariably followed by an Indian Meal, a 'lock-in' if possible in our local, then off to bed to do it all again the next day. I guess our only restriction was the lack of funds to pay for the decadent lifestyle. I remember our standby drink was 'VPs' wine at 10s 6d a bottle from the Off Licence, not to be recommended unless desperate!

If our introduction to the 'homosexual' world was a bit of a shock in Eastney, life in Britannia was every bit as open, particularly when the Royal Household was embarked. None of this was a problem for us newbies other than a tad confusing as it was not meant to take place at all under military law. Looking back, it was an open secret and nobody really chose to notice. Quite right.

The RMSM, Portsmouth Group and HMS Excellent bands in a memorable orchestral concert in Portsmouth Guildhall sometime in 1970. I was sat next to the *Leader* BdSgt Chris Shepherd.
Conductors Lt Col Paul Neville, Capt Tom Lambert, Lt Chris Taylor.
Piano soloist Michael Roll in Mozart's Piano Concerto No 23 in A (K488).

CHAPTER 7

The Royal Yacht Britannia

My early days in Eastney were spent mainly getting myself organised with uniforms and kit ready to deploy in Britannia to sail on 15th October 1968. The Drum Major of the Yacht Band was Drum Major Colin Bowden, a highly respected leader and charming man (who became a good friend in later life) whose skills included, among many others, an in-depth knowledge of Big Band music about which he entertained the ship's company over the ship's radio with his favourites. By the way, he was an excellent Drum Major in front of the band too! Colin had high standards and was good with us new boys (we were considered boys until we reached the age of 18) making us feel welcome. He made sure we understood what we needed to take with us, especially the tropical uniforms which we had not seen before. Importantly for me, Colin insisted that I applied to become a candidate for promotion immediately on joining the band, a move that gave me extra seniority as a candidate for promotion at a time when promotion was less fashionable than it subsequently became. I was even selected, at the tender age of 19 years, to undertake a Junior Command Course (the military 6-week course) to qualify as a Band Corporal in October 1970. I was promoted Band Corporal at the age of 22 years - unheard of in the modern age, but not so unusual at that time.

The Bandmaster was Warrant Officer Bandmaster Johnny Masters who was a straight-talking kind-hearted man who wanted the best for us. He imparted many solid values in us and I got along just fine with him. I always remember Johnny saying to me some time later, "Never start something that the person who follows you cannot also do." Although a fairly negative

The Royal Yacht Band - Madeira October 1968
John's very first gig on the Royal Yacht - Cornet third from right.
Behind John is John Hillier on piccolo.

approach, it did have more merit at this time, such was the fluid nature of moving personnel between different bands. Disruption has happened less down the years and 'drafting' turbulence is kept to a minimum in the modern era, mostly happening because of promotion or on request.

A few other members of the band I had known from time in training, albeit they were a little older than me. John Hillier (who in later life became the Director of Music Captain John Hillier MBE) the flautist was an early pal and we have remained good friends to this day. John was my best man and I was his. We shared many a run ashore - and still do! My 'sea-daddy' was Band Corporal Rodney Preston, a fellow violinist who was tasked to keep me fit to play and away from all the temptations confronting a young man travelling abroad - he failed in this regard, but succeeded in every other way! We became great friends and Rodney introduced me to a whole repertoire of music through his recorded music that passed many an hour at sea. We still meet a couple of times each year

John in Barbados
West Indies 1968.
Ashore in Royal Yacht Band
Ceremonial Tunic

and chat over the unique experiences we shared in Britannia. Rodney looked after me over the next few years as we shared the Band Cabin/Music Library together which was a seriously good 'perk'. The Band Cabin, although tiny, became our sleeping quarters as well as the instrument storage and music library - most importantly it was mid-ships and, as I soon discovered on leaving Portsmouth en route for Madeira through the Bay of Biscay, I was a terrible sailor. Really terrible!

As many will know, sea-sickness is awful as you cannot get away from it. For me, big ships are better than small ships and Britannia, being only 5862 tonnes (*see Appendix One* for Facts and Figures about Britannia), was one of the worst. Its design caused it to corkscrew up and down in any sort of choppy sea and it was worse at the bow end of the ship, coincidentally where the band accommodation was located. To make things worse, until a major refit in late 1969, there were no fitted bunks for the Band or the RM detachment of seven Royal Marines Commandos who shared the same accommodation. There was only one space further forward than the Band Mess which was the Junior Rates Recreation space and bar, where all ratings under the rank of Petty Officer met and socialised (smoked and drank beer mostly) and watched the nightly film. It was only after the film was finished that the band could access this space to assemble your camp bed (yes, the old-fashioned type of rods and canvass) to finally get some sleep - this was rarely before 11pm. The smell of stale beer and cigarettes is never forgotten and there was nothing worse if you suffer from sea-sickness. All this was a real shock to the system and was not what I was expecting in my mind's eye prior to joining. In fact space was so limited for every activity it was a miracle we stowed everything in order to perform our professional jobs. However, we did, and it worked incredibly well for 44 years which is testament to the quality and ingenuity of Yachtsmen who took immense pride in what they were doing.

The crew of Royal Yachtsmen were volunteers from the general service of the Royal Navy. Officers were appointed for up to two years, while the yachtsmen were drafted as volunteers and after 365 days service could be admitted to 'The Permanent Royal Yacht Service'. As Royal Yachtsmen they served until they chose to leave the Royal Yacht Service or were dismissed for medical or disciplinary reasons. When I joined Britannia in 1968 there were a number of the crew who had been serving onboard since Britannia was commissioned in 1954! What this achieved was to create a bank of expertise within the crew that can only be achieved by experience and commitment to the job. This I found inspiring and I too quickly became one of the same.

By the way, The Naval Discipline Act did not apply to those serving in Britannia, the only punishments being a 'warning' or to be 'Dismissed Royal Yacht Service'. This happened from time to time, in the band as well, which caused extra problems as everyone played a specific musical instrument of which there was generally only one player in each category. At times like this a replacement had to be flown out to join us, or we just made do if a replacement was not feasible. Long-haul flights were difficult to justify in those days.

Band Royal Duties

Me, Alan Upton and Dick Grainger on trumpets. John Cockwill bass, Alan Flook percussion. Typical of many impromptu entertainments on the foc'sle.

The Band's principal tasks included playing music onboard for lunches, dinners, church services, cocktail parties, dances and ships entertainments. Most of the formal functions took place in the Royal Apartments in the aft quarters of the ship. The band, or more usually the orchestra, would set up as soon as the signal was given that the Royal Party had moved from the Drawing Room to the Dining Room when the 'chair-party' would quickly carry the folding chairs up the stairs to the Ante-Room area for the orchestra to set up. The music and instruments were carried by the players, the whole exercise taking just a couple of minutes, so by the time guests were seated we had appeared as if by magic and had started to play our first piece (normally a lively march).

Music programmes were selected well in advance of the trip and submitted to the Palace for clearance to prevent any possible gaffe with an inappropriate title. The format of the formal music programmes remained the same throughout my time, with a typical sequence being: March, Overture, Waltz, 3 x light popular classics, a selection of show tunes, a solo item, and fillers as required.

Informal nights at sea differed from formal functions when the Royal Family were embarked in Britannia. We would still play background music albeit the atmosphere was less formal and light-hearted, even to the point where tricks might be played within the family. One such occasion was when Lord Louis Mountbatten was travelling with The Queen. Lord Mountbatten had many anecdotes about pieces of music, especially marches which he prided himself as somewhat of an expert as to their origins. One night we were passed a note by a senior Royal to switch the march to something other than the march printed in the programme of music placed on the dining table. This we did, yet Lord Louis embarked on a detailed story about the march listed in the programme unaware that we had made the switch. All very amusing for everyone other than Lord Louis!

Ashore we would play for all the above functions when held in Embassies, plus flag-waving, school and community events. This in itself led to a rare assortment of gigs, such as taking our equipment ashore on ship's boats to Pitcairn Island in the middle of the South Pacific, and confusing the Islanders with a marching display. There were many such performances in unlikely places and the unusual was the norm for the Yacht Band. The Royal Marines term 'adapt and overcome' was never more apt.

The Yacht was a regular sight at Cowes Week in early August and, usually, for the remainder of the month, was home to the Queen and her family for an annual cruise around the islands off the West coast of Scotland (known as the 'Western Isles Trip'). The Royal Family were completely at home in Britannia and relaxed in a way not possible elsewhere. It took new Yachties some time to get used to the fact that every day was an exceptional day with Royalty and major overseas visitors in attendance. After a while this became second nature and we almost stopped noticing, a bit like New York (Manhattan) where, for the last 12 years, we have visited family twice each year and hardly looked up at the skyline after the first few visits.

In my time serving in Britannia, major visits included:

Portugal, Norway, West Indies (most Islands numerous times), Panama City and Canal, Brazil, Mexico, British Honduras, USA, Canada, South Africa, North Africa, Suez Canal, Mediterranean and Islands, Malaysia, Thailand, Borneo, Sri Lanka, Australia, New Zealand, New Guinea, South Pacific – including Fiji, Samoa, Tonga, Bora Bora. Easter Island, Galapagos Islands, Pitcairn Island, Soloman Islands, Tahiti, Hawaii, Western Islands of the UK.

The Queen being piped onboard
Always happiest in Britannia
© *Crown copyright*

CHAPTER 8

Learning Curve

My first months in Britannia were not particularly happy ones and it took me some time to find my feet. Yes, there were lots of memorable and fun times visiting places such as Madeira, Barbados, Rio de Janeiro, Recife, but life onboard was less fun for me in the early days. Apart from the frequent sea-sickness there was a daily routine of living in such close quarters which was hard to adjust to arriving straight from training. As mentioned earlier, Tot (daily rum ration) was the central point of each day on the mess deck and in general terms the UA members of the band, of which I think there were three of us, were not welcome in the Mess while the 'men' were drinking. Tot time led to cans (normally by the crate) of beer appearing from the bar (there being no limit on the amount of beer one could buy unlike the ration on warships) which prolonged the session well into the afternoon. The result was a virtual 'no-go' area for those of us too young to be part of the revelries. It was difficult as the options to go elsewhere were limited to the few areas of the upper deck available to the ship's company. Often us UAs would be plied with a sip or two of rum, which was well meant I'm sure, but for me it was not welcome as I couldn't stand the stuff. Still can't!

Over time I found a way around this awkward time of the day as I identified a cabin, used by one of the Royal Secretaries when the Royal Family were embarked, to use to practice the violin. This area was in the Royal Apartments and almost deserted before the Royals embarked, so quite by chance I had an area I could use to practice, read and relax; a real life-saver. Everyone got used to me being there so this proved a major upturn in my fortunes, plus I could practice. I would head back to the RM Mess later in the afternoon when the lunchtime session was over and sleep was the predominant activity! Marvellous. I never liked rum and I never liked Tot time. For me 31st July 1970 was a positive change to life onboard although there was much sorrow in many quarters, yet it was still two years away!

There were plenty of like-minded folk in the band and, believe it or not, five salvationists[7], if you include me as a somewhat lost soul in this regard by now. John Thorne (cornet and violin), Terry Toon (cornet and violin), Rodney Williamson (euphonium and cello) and Dave Miles (cornet and piano). Rodney Williamson was a Band Corporal at this time and he would go on to become a Warrant Officer First Class and Bandmaster of The Band of The Britannia Royal Naval College at Dartmouth. He later became The Corps Bandmaster at the Royal Marines School of Music in 1984. Rodney was a clever man and recognised my unhappy state of mind, and took me under his wing. I always remember him telling me that the way to get along with

---

[7] Salvationists, being tee-total, left their rum tot for others to drink, prolonging the lunchtime sessions to the delight of many!

others in ships was to learn everyone's Christian name so you would have them at a disadvantage. What wise words, how true and a tip that served me well down the years. We remained friends for many years.

Dave Miles had no ambitions for promotion, but was certainly one of the best pianists to have served in the Royal Marines Band Service. Years of accompanying others in the Salvation Army as a child had given him a grounding in sight-reading[8] which was exceptional and he had the technique to go with it, regularly performing as a soloist. A terrific performance in Portsmouth Guildhall of the 'Scherzo' by Litolff (sometime in 1969 I think) comes to mind. The thing about David I liked most was that he was a worse cornet player than me, therefore made me look good - thanks Dave! Dave left us in the early 1970s to join The RAF Central Band as their accompanist where he stayed as a single instrument player until retiring at pensionable age. The RAF definitely had the best of that deal.

It's funny how negative experiences can be a valuable source of knowledge in later life. I remember the low point for me of this first trip was a marching display we were giving in The British Embassy grounds in Rio De Janeiro as part of a Royal Cocktail party. The steady buildup of discontent in recent weeks was getting the better of me and it only took something small to tip me over the edge. I'd had enough and was off! Or so I thought. I was spotted by a SNCO who again became Bandmaster of the Yacht Band a few years later, John Gould (French Horn). John sensed my departure from the assembly area and followed me, eventually talking

Members of The Royal Yacht Band - St Lucia West Indies January 1970
Right to left: Rodney Preston, Paddy Mailey, Dave Miles, Charlie Soloman
How the other half live!

---

[8] Including playing fluently from a full score adding the missing parts as required. Particularly useful with small orchestra work.

me down to earth again and putting things in perspective. I think this was probably followed up by a meeting of the leadership of the band to improve the life of the newbies in the band, regardless of how well they were handling the music. I drew upon my negative experiences in later years throughout my time as Director of Music and always tried to have my antenna finely tuned to recognise problems in others, especially the youngsters.

As with everything in life, we learn to adapt to our situation over time and overcome minor difficulties (adapt and overcome). Within a year or so I was far more comfortable with life onboard and felt I was a key member of the band. I enjoyed many a 'run ashore' with John Hillier and another old friend Jeremy Tugwood, the three of us getting into all manner of scrapes, all harmless, but great fun. Jeremy was a little older and a Band Corporal so he should have known better, so I blame him. The least said about Panama City the better…..! Jeremy had a long and distinguished career in Britannia going on to become the Bandmaster of the Yacht Band in the late 1970s. In fact the whole band was a very social group and a party was always just around the corner throughout my time in Britannia.

Similarly, the sense of humour in the Band Service is legendary and it was simply not possible to take yourself too seriously. Any form of pomposity was quickly snuffed out and humility was, and is, the overriding trait of Royal Marines musicians[9]. So much so I believe they do not realise quite how good many of them are, being so quick at self-deprecation. In later life I was tasked with managing an Armed Forces Music Bursary Scheme which sponsored University/ Music College students through a degree programme on the understanding that they would come and join us on leaving college. Part of this process was to assess each of the students twice yearly. It opened my eyes as to the wide range of abilities in civilian music institutions, with the majority of students I saw being totally ill-prepared to join the Royal Marines Band Service even after achieving a performance music degree. It was a fairly disastrous scheme which was eventually - and rightly - dropped. But it did bring into sharp focus the need to retain a military School of Music, where a thorough music training could be delivered and assessed to ensure a common standard was maintained. I am pleased to say that this remains the case 24 years after I was Director of Music Training.

There has always been a mix of abilities within the Band Service, and occasionally there are some who are not suited to the life of a professional Military musician. I myself have encouraged a few musicians to leave the service down the years believing they were in the wrong environment to make the best of their skills and achieve a successful career. I have been pleased how many thanked me years later as it was the nudge they needed to prosper in a completely different career. Often it is nobody's fault because natural talent plays such a big part in outcomes. However, the success rate is high and there have been countless numbers of

---

[9] Some musicians in civilian life could learn from this!

superb musicians come through the RM Music system and go on to be leading figures in civilian life after serving in the Royal Marines Band Service. Look no further than the world-class horn virtuoso and teacher Frank Lloyd who was with us for ten years, mostly as Principal Horn of the Staff Band at Deal. For many years the Armed forces was the biggest employer of musicians in the country and is probably only second to the BBC today in the number employed. How many communities have benefited from having these highly training individuals go on to a second career in teaching and working in the civilian music profession. A priceless contribution to the quality of life in the UK, which is hard to quantify in financial terms.

Frank Lloyd returning to the RMSM in April 1982 to play
Webber's Concertino for Horn and Orchestra in E minor, Op. 45
A stunning performance - as usual from Frank!
One of my final concerts with the Staff Orchestra before
moving to Higher Training

CHAPTER 9

1969 - A Year to Remember

Opportunities that got away

A big moment for me in early 1969 was a realisation that I was not entirely comfortable with my level of violin playing (having only been playing the instrument for a little over three years) and I needed to get lessons if I were to make further progress. Everyone was happy with my playing at work and I had played two concertos (one being Mozart's 2nd Violin Concerto in D) with the orchestra already, as well as leading the orchestra for Sir Vivian Dunn's final concert in Portsmouth, a concert that was littered with violin solos. However, I knew I could do more, so I requested the Director of Music (Captain Tom Lambert - he wasn't all bad!) to fund some lessons for me. To my surprise, he not only funded the lessons, but arranged for me to have railway warrants to travel to London every second Monday to have lessons with Molly Mack at The Royal Academy of Music (RAM). Thus started a 3-year period when I travelled to the RAM when in England to have lessons with Molly, a highly respected teacher on the London scene. This was just what I needed and I worked my way through some of the concerto repertoire as well as spending much time improving my bowing technique.

I also had the good fortune to contact an ex-RMB percussionist and former member of the Portsmouth Band named Mac Macintosh. 'Mac' was now working in the music library at Saddlers Wells Opera company during the day, and an usher in the Dress Circle at English National Opera (ENO) in the evenings. Mac offered me accommodation in London when I could stay overnight on Mondays after my lesson, and he also let me slip into the good seats at ENO to listen to operas, hitherto, an area of music I had never been exposed to. What a bonus. I saw a whole range of operas during this time from the Mozart, Verdi and Puccini classics to Stravinsky's 'The Rakes Progress' and Prokofiev's 'The Love of Three Oranges' and more. I think this exposure to great singing gave me a love of choral music which is as strong today as ever.

Another spin-off of the lessons with Molly were (by her recommendation) auditions arranged with the Leader of The Bournemouth Symphony Orchestra (Brendan O'Brian) and The Hallé Orchestra in Manchester (Martin Milner). By late 1969 my interest in playing the trumpet had diminished and I was passionate about getting into an orchestra and playing orchestral music rather than the military/concert band repertoire.

In August that year The Portsmouth Band was tasked to take part in the NATO Tattoo in Arnhem Holland for three weeks. I knew there was a professional orchestra based in Arnhem so I contacted the Leader of the Arnhem Philharmonic Orchestra (via The British Consulate) to ask whether he might have time to give me a couple of lessons during our visit for the tattoo. He agreed, so I took my violin and met The Leader (Mr KoeKoe) on arrival. He was a terrific man and got me working on using my fingers on my bowing hand far more than I was doing. This was achieved through a set of exercises and studies that were repetitive and used to develop muscle memory so the process became second nature. I got on very well with Mr KoeKoe and he must have seen enough talent in me to offer me a place in the Arnhem Orchestra living with him and his family for one year as a probation period to make sure both parties were happy for something more permanent. What an opportunity, and a little more 'exotic' than staying in England! He even gave me a parting present of a 'Hills[10]' chin rest which I use to this day. The chin rest was one of three given to Mr KoeKoe by the great Russian violinist David Oistrakh, my absolute favourite player in the second half of the twentieth Century. There is no way to prove its provenance, but there is also no reason to doubt it. It remains very special to me.

The thing about Tattoos is that, once rehearsed, they run for days or weeks with no further rehearsal. Just get there for the performance[11], in the case of Arnhem once per night - no matinee. This allowed plenty of free time to get up to mischief which was led by the fact that 'Gordons' gin was a mere 9s 6d a litre bottle - 45p in today's money. I think all of us young men did our best to kill ourselves with the stuff and it was some years before I could say yes to a Gin & Tonic - at least a decade! My only other memory of The Arnhem Tattoo was that they fed us three meals each day, all of which were basically yogurt!

Anyway, back to the story. Reality kicked in when I applied for my discharge to take one of these orchestral career paths to be told that discharge was not possible other than on medical or disciplinary grounds. This was well before the days when the option to purchase your discharge or give notice became a right.

My disappointments were short-lived as there was still much about my life in the Band Service that I liked, such as Royal Yacht service[12], mates, music and travel, and a conversation with my old violin teacher Harry Lipman helped. Harry crystallised the situation by saying, "You are better off being a big fish in a small pond rather than a small fish in a big pond." And so it has proved.

---

[10] Starting with Joseph Hill (b-1715-84) The London based Hill family became the foremost experts in the world of violins.

[11] We often went over to Richmond Park to play golf during the day when in London for the Royal Tournament. Perfect!

[12] A major 5-month world tour to Australia and New Zealand was planned for early the next year.

CHAPTER 10

Performance Jitters

There are countless stories of how nerves can affect musicians (or performers generally) and many talented musicians have been blighted by the onset of nerves or the 'pearlies' as it is sometimes called in the profession. I have good friends today who I know to be superb musicians yet cannot seem to bring their best to the concert platform because of nerves. They suffer big-time when they have every skill you could possibly wish to have. Once the 'pearlies' start it is hard to control and many a career has been cut short, or limited by this. I mention this here because three events in 1969 provided me with experiences to manage nerves and use them in a positive way.

The first was during a Royal Visit to Norway later in 1969. The Royal Family embarked in Britannia on 4th August in Hull and Britannia set sail for The Shetland Isles, where amongst other things The Queen was presented with an elaborately printed (with some gold leaf) musical tune for folk violin. This was in turn passed to Captain Tom Lambert our Director of Music to make sense of and prepare it for a performance later in the cruise. In a break with tradition the Royal Family decided not to use Britannia for either Cowes Week or the Western Isles Cruise, deciding instead to go on a cruise of the Norwegian Fjords with the Norwegian Royal Family who were embarked in their Royal Yacht 'Norge'. On arrival in Norway King Olav, Crown Prince Harold and Crown Princess Sonja joined Britannia for passage into Bergen. After formalities in Bergen[13] on day one of the visit, both Royal Families continued on in Britannia for a few days sight-seeing around the Fjords.

It was after dinner one evening that myself (violin) and Dave Miles (piano) were tasked to await the Royal Party in the Drawing Room (which has a decent baby grand piano) to perform this folk tune which had been gifted to The Queen the previous week. To say I was a little nervous is an understatement, as hitherto I had always been part of the larger orchestra or band, thereby being relatively invisible, but tonight there was no hiding place. To his credit Tom Lambert was there to chaperone us and he did put us at our ease, although to be fair I never saw Dave Miles anything other than totally relaxed all the time I knew him! When the Royal Party came through to the Drawing Room it was a stunning sight with all the Royals from both families, and members of both their extended families all dressed in their evening dress - spectacular. I was holding my violin ready to play and remember feeling that I had never played the instrument before, such was the level of tension I was feeling. However, as ever, The Royals were superb, and with a few choice words from The Queen (who appeared very keen to hear the result of this folk tune gift) and Prince Philip I was ready to go. It was not a difficult piece and it was over

---

[13] Where incidentally Cay was on a school trip at the same time!

almost before it had begun. Polite applause followed and we were done. Looking back to this night it was a terrific memory to retain to put nerves in perspective. If you could manage the situation in front of two Royal Families (in a small room) and still produce a good result, other less pressured situations should be a doddle!

The second notable event was the annual Festival of Remembrance broadcast live on television over Remembrance weekend in November 1969. The producer of the Festival at this time was William Henry Ralph Reader CBE (who was very tactile and kept cuddling me, all very alarming!), a larger than life character, famous for his 'Scouting' activities, who was a little overpowering for a young lad such as me. For the finale of the Festival, part of the Henry Wood Sea Songs were to be played ending with Rule Britannia and including all the national songs which are so famous because of Last Night of The Proms. Ralph had decided that the hornpipe should be played on the violin, in traditional manner. I was volunteered by Captain Tom Lambert to be the violinist. Although not the most demanding of pieces to play, it was nevertheless a very lonely feeling standing centre stage in The Royal Albert Hall to play a solo on live television, with what I sensed was a less than supportive group of Army musicians surrounding me. There has always been a healthy rivalry between the three music services which comes to the fore on occasions such as The Festival of Remembrance. Anyway, having heard a few derogatory comments from musicians on the stage behind me, I decided to 'warm up' by playing a little of the Mendelssohn Violin Concerto, possibly to illustrate that the sailors' hornpipe was not my only tune. This had the desired effect to silence any potential critics behind me and the show went well. I realised then and there that I did not need universal praise and 'lashings' of encouragement to do well, as I could manage that by myself, a lesson I always remembered - back yourself.

The third was a solo I played as an extra item after dinner in the Royal Yacht Wardroom Mess when the officers were dining out Queen Elizabeth The Queen Mother. It was customary for the Wardroom (Officers) Mess to hold a formal dining evening on Saturdays when at sea. On such occasions when the Royals were embarked they would invite a member of the family to be their special guest for the evening. One such evening at sea with The Queen Mother in attendance I was nominated to play an 'extra item' as an after-dinner solo. I had chosen a Gypsy piece named 'Gypsy Carnival'[14]. We had rehearsed this piece in the morning in the Recreation Space as was our normal practice and all was well. However, when it came to the real thing I was introduced and stepped forward to play over the polite applause. This particular solo has a slow introduction with all manner of slips and slides up and down the fingerboard. The start was fairly catastrophic as during the first 'up bow' the tip of my bow hit the Deck-head (ceiling) causing me to almost drop the bow. I heard a couple of gasps from the diners who had spotted what had happened and I immediately bent my knees a few inches to lower my overall height.

---

[14] I have seen the same piece with a slightly different title.

For those who haven't tried this, believe me, it hurts! By this time I was on auto-pilot with the music and just had to concentrate like mad to maintain the lower position for the next six minutes or so. At the end of my ordeal the applause was rapturous and clearly not for the music, but for my heroic knee bend!

The next day I was called to the door of the Royal Marines Mess Deck as I had a visitor. On arrival at the door I was met by The Queen Mother who said (words to the effect of), "Musician Perkins, I just wanted to stop by and say how much we all enjoyed your solo last night. Thank you." And with that, she was gone!

Another lesson for a life in music is, 'adapt and overcome' because the best laid plans don't always work as you might hope and there is so much that can trip you up. In fact musicians rarely talk about the successful concerts, preferring to relive the things that didn't go to plan - disasters are so much more memorable!

In truth I have also learned that the audience is always on your side and wants you to do well. Why else would they have bought a ticket?

Odds and Ends

Talking about things that can go wrong!

Every September the Portsmouth Band had a very nice week on the Bandstand in Howard Davis Park St Helier, Jersey. This was a plum gig when there were no Yacht trips so everyone was available to take part. We stayed in hotel accommodation close to the park and the daily routine was to play on the Bandstand once during the day and once during the evening. After each evening performance we would change into our marching uniform and perform a 'Beating Retreat' ceremony with the traditional evening hymn, Sunset, Rule Britannia and so on. We always aimed to be in the pub by 10pm!

On the final evening's concert it became a tradition to play Tchaikovsky's 1812 Overture with all the pyrotechnics, for which we transported galvanised dustbins in which to set the 'stage' explosives. In charge of pyrotechnics this particular year was BdCSgt Bob Loft (RIP) who was no stranger to things going pear-shaped! Bob had devised a complex plan of setting the explosives back behind the audience on the tree line. His train of thought was that in the darkness of the late evening the effect would be more dramatic than the tried and tested location of behind the Bandstand. This particular year (I think 1969) had been a dry summer and the park was a little like a tinder box just waiting for our musical arsonist to appear. Towards the end of the 1812 Bob worked his magic with the pyrotechnics and the first explosion set light to a large tree which burst into flames and quickly transferred to an adjoining tree and so on....

It was dark apart from safety lighting around the footpaths and the audience (and us) were shocked and a general panic kicked off! More explosions caused further chaos around the tree line and from our vantage point of the Bandstand it looked amazing! Over a few stressful final chords of the 1812 the Fire Brigade arrived and calm was restored. I have never played the 1812 Overture since without my mind wandering back to that night in Howard Davis Park all those years ago. The best performance ever!

Coming up in 1970. My favourite trip during my time in Britannia.

The Royal Tournament Fanfare Team 1977
Massed bands rehearsals on South Barracks sports field RMSM Deal.
L to R: Jock Milne, Jon Yates, ???, Ray Moseley, Jan Zavada, John Perkins, Alan Upton, Ian Naylor, Dave Stockham, Keith Sivyer. *Sitting down:* Terry Wood, Dave Cole

CHAPTER 11

Captain Cook's Bicentennial Tour 1970

If 1969 had been a year of short trips, 1970 was a different beast altogether. We set sail on 19th January to begin a long deployment to the Southern Hemisphere and were due to be away for over 5 months. The voyage was mainly to mark the 200th Anniversary of Captain Cook's first voyage of discovery in the Pacific Ocean, culminating in a re-enactment of Cook's first landing in Botany Bay on 29th April. A key part of this trip was to visit The Galapagos Islands en route and visit many of the Islands Cook himself discovered, where a fondness for the Royal Family was passionate. Essential supplies for Britannia to carry were 50,000 cans of beer and 400 gallons of rum! I don't think we brought much back. Hoorah!

The blue-footed booby is perhaps the most famous of the Galapagos birds

Although Royal Duty was the highlight of any trip, these duties only started when The Royals embarked in Britannia. The time before and after were ideal for the Ship's Company to enjoy many a good 'run ashore' and enjoy Britannia's upper decks for sun-bathing and sports. On these long trips, this meant weeks rather than days and it was a real bonus visiting various countries for refuelling whilst en route. It wasn't until 4th March that The Queen and Royal Party embarked for the main purpose of the trip. Before then we had visited Madeira, Barbados, Christobel and The Panama Canal on 8th February. A few days later we arrived off Tower Island which is part of the Galapagos Islands. We were given unrestricted access to these islands, long before they became popular destinations for tourists. This unspoiled remote spot was quite unlike anywhere else on earth. The birds and wildlife were unthreatened by humans and had no fear of us whatsoever. The giant Tortoises are fascinating and the seas were full of exotic marine life that you could observe closeup. An amazing place which we were to visit again in future years.

The Galapagos Giant Tortoise can live for more than 100 years, the oldest recorded tortoise being 152 years old.

The Marine Iguana is the only lizard in the world with the ability to live and forage at sea and is endemic to the Galapagos

After a day or two on Galapagos us lucky travellers resumed our voyage stopping at Tahiti, Bora Bora and Palmerston Island, before arriving in Lutoka, Fiji on 2nd March for the start of Royal Duty two days later.

Royal Duty began formally in Suva (the capital of Fiji) where the Queen received the traditional invitation to land from seven Fijian Chiefs before embarking on a full programme of formal engagements culminating in a State Dinner in the evening. It was always the case that when leaving a port the Royal Marines Band would be on the Royal Deck (the highest point in Britannia) to play national tunes and popular songs as an entertainment whilst leaving. Often this would be reciprocated by a local band on shore alternating between us and them with their songs. Fiji was the most memorable of all these departures for me as the massed singers sang the Fijian song of farewell 'Isa Lei'. This was totally magical from onboard Britannia as the sight and sounds faded into the distance. Wow, unlike anywhere else we visited.

The next stop was Tonga where The King, King Taufa 'ahau Tupou IV, a larger than life man in every respect, hosted the Queen for another full day of official engagements. This included a Tongan feast of roast suckling pigs, chickens, lobsters and fruit. Many of us were still onboard Britannia when a lorry load of the same food arrived as a gift to the ship's company which was distributed between the Mess decks. The most memorable part was a number of roasted pigs heads which were alarming to say the least, although a few of our numbers gave them a go; mind you it was after 'tot' time! At the end of a busy programme in Tonga the Yacht sailed in total silence watching 3000 children holding torches along the shoreline, making for another magical leaving harbour, quite unlike anywhere else we had been to.

Sydney Harbour 1970
The Opera House was still under construction in 1970. The band was given a private tour of the building during our visit.

45

CHAPTER 12

New Zealand

Most people who visit New Zealand find an England of yesteryear with its green and rolling landscape and neatly kept gardens and a South Island similar in parts to the highlands of Scotland. The weather is much the same as the UK, albeit differing greatly from a sub-tropical in the far north to a chilly south. Our first landfall was the capital Wellington which is sited at the southern tip of the North Island. A clever local journalist had discovered that we had three notorious Outlaws (only in name!) in the band in Tom Mailey, 'Polly' Perkins and 'Ned' Kelly (RIP), the most infamous of all. The local papers were full of this story and the band was tasked to play in a number of places around the city where the 'three outlaws' story was the headline each time. In fact Ned Kelly was retiring from the Band Service after this trip to become a school teacher (eventually a Head Teacher), his specialist subject being Geography. Ned practised his teaching on me and I managed an 'A' grade GCE Geography on return to the UK - thanks Ned!

A Disastrous Crossing

Wellington was a terrific start to our New Zealand tour. The weather was great and we had a good number of gigs ashore. It was always nice to get out and about to see something of the place, which was one of the spin-off benefits of being in the band. However, overnight on 14th March the winds picked up and the weather changed dramatically, coinciding with our scheduled departure in the early hours for the short hop across the Cook Straits to Picton on South Island. On leaving the harbour entrance the Yacht was hit by a huge wave that swamped the foc'sle and trapped the First Lieutenant in the bow of the ship. The Anchor Party had been surprised by this deluge of water which put all their lives in peril. It wasn't for some considerable time, during which period the First Lieutenant was hanging on for his life, that the water pressure was reduced by opening the foc'sle doors, thus recovering everyone. The New Zealand escort ship HMNZS Waikato wasn't as lucky as three men working on the foc'sle were swept overboard as the same wave hit them. The weather conditions prevented a return back to Wellington, so Waikato had to wait until it had passed through the narrow strait before her Wasp helicopter could be launched to affect a rescue. With great skill, the helicopter crew managed to rescue two of the three overboard, but sadly the third was not saved. Once conditions eased Waikato turned back for Wellington while Britannia continued across the Cook Straits on to Picton.

This was the roughest sea I have been in either before or since and quite terrifying for everyone, not least because the Queen and Prince Philip were embarked. Although I was sleeping in the Band Cabin, which is midships and more stable, everything on the shelves tipped off, the angle of the list being so extreme. It appeared impossible to stand up and my admiration for the seamen who were able to function throughout this ordeal rocketed. Looking back, this whole episode could have turned out much worse as only two years earlier, in the same place, in a similar storm, the sinking of the Lyttelton–Wellington ferry 'Wahine' on 10 April 1968 was New Zealand's worst modern maritime disaster. Fifty-one people lost their lives that day, another died several weeks later.

Back on Schedule

Relative calm returned to the schedule after the infamous crossing of the Cook Straits with visits to Lyttleton (the sea port for Christchurch), Timaru and Dunedin, before picking up the Captain Cook Trail once again in Napier and Gisborne. The city of Gisborne stands on the site where Captain Cook first landed in New Zealand to a hostile reception from the Maoris on 8th October 1769. Further visits north to Tauranga and Mercury Bay where Captain Cook set up a shore station to observe the transit of the planet Mercury on 9th November 1769. Captain Cook's landing was reenacted for the benefit of the Royal Party, before heading to New Zealand's most populous city Auckland.

The arrival in Auckland was spectacular with a large Amanda of craft sailing out to welcome Britannia and escort her into port. The welcome party was so large that it needed over one hundred control boats just to manage them. The impact was spectacular, achieving what only Her Majesty sailing in Britannia (fully 'dressed' and band playing) could achieve; worldwide media coverage and a huge positive for Great Britain PLC. No other nation could come close to the impact of Britannia arriving on a State visit.

Over the three days in Auckland the Band members had plenty of time to get out and explore the city, which was an impressive place for a 19-year-old. The people were very friendly and there was a ready welcome in all the pubs for anyone in uniform. During a significant part of the 20th century, New Zealand hotels/pubs shut their public bars at 6pm. A culture of heavy drinking, the 'six o'clock swill' (or 'the bums rush' as it was better known), developed during the time between finishing work at 5pm and the mandatory closing time only an hour later. This six o'clock closing was introduced during the First World War, partly as an attempt to improve public morality and partly as a war austerity measure. It was made permanent in 1919 owing to pressure from the then powerful temperance movement. While the new law was supposed to curb drunkenness and crime and to send men home early to encourage family life, in practice it had the opposite effect. It created a culture of binge drinking where men would finish work at 5pm and had only one hour to drink as much alcohol as possible before closing. In a national referendum in 1967 voters supported a move to ten o'clock closing - and the 'swill' ended on 9th October 1967. This binge culture was still very evident when we arrived in 1970 and wearing a military uniform with Royal Yacht badges when ashore attracted plenty of well-meaning drinkers who invited us to join them. Oh dear!

On leaving Auckland we sailed north for the Easter Weekend to Waitangi and The Bay of Islands, a mini paradise with a sub-tropical climate and beautiful scenery, especially when approached by sea. New Zealand was a revelation in many ways and lived up to the glowing reports I had read about the lifestyle and beauty of the place. Us Brits were made to feel very welcome everywhere we travelled and the combination of a generous male drinking population and welcoming NZ girls seemed too good to be true! I think by the time we left for Australia I had already formulated a long-term plan to find a way back there, possibly to the New Zealand Broadcasting Orchestra[15], which we had heard during our visit.

Jackstay Transfers at Sea

One of the most exhilarating (and scary) activities at sea is transferring between ships via a Jackstay Transfer roping system. We would transfer to the escort frigates at times to play a concert for them. The light jackstay is used for transferring personnel, provisions, and stores. The hauling end of the jackstay is manned by up to 25 hands. The other end is secured by a grommet strop to slip in the receiving ship. Working distance limits between ships are up to 24 to 61 metres with a normal working distance of about 34 metres. It is obviously critical that the ships maintain the speed and course to remain the exact distance apart. For many years the transfer of provisions and even people at sea was done by the use of jackstay lines between ships, but this is a skill that for the most part has been replaced by the use of a ship's sea boats and embarked helicopters. As a result, the use of jackstay lines is rarely used. However, it was commonplace during my time in Britannia.

Playing background music for
refuelling at sea

John hanging around!

---

[15] Some years later I applied for my discharge to join one of the ABC orchestras (Melbourne, Sydney or Perth) in Australia. My discharge request was refused as I had to give a return of service after completing The Bandmasters' Course.

CHAPTER 13

Australia

On 3rd April we arrived in Australia and the start of another new adventure for me. There is nothing quite like doing something for the first time, especially when you are young and possibilities are endless. Our first stop was Hobart in Tasmania. We had been told by the more seasoned travellers to expect Australia to be more like the USA than New Zealand which was very much like England. Having not been to the USA I had little to go on, but my first impression of Tasmania was that of a rather dreary place. This was not helped by the poor weather which made our few musical engagements touch and go, so it was with enthusiasm that we sailed for Melbourne two days later. Melbourne was altogether different and a real gem of a city. My main recollection was going to the 'Musos' Club one evening to listen to the Jacques Loussier Trio playing their jazz take on Bach. Magnificent to listen to such skill in a small intimate room, and a real eye opener that someone could have such original ideas. All in all, Melbourne was a big 'thumbs up'.

Next we sailed back down the Yarra River to visit Port Kembla, Newcastle, Coff's Harbour and Brisbane where the yacht received another spectacular entry with around 250,000 people lining the banks and countless small craft escorting Britannia to her berth. There is a tried and tested

The Royal Yacht Band 1970 *(less our two offenders from the Brisbane marching display)*
with Flag Officer Royal Yachts (FORY)
John third from left in middle row

49

system for entering harbour which entails (amongst many other traditions) the RM Band performing on The Royal Deck and playing suitable music to entertain both the ship's company and any escorting vessels and media. It creates a striking impact. I remember this entering harbour very clearly as it was almost 40 degrees with no shade and we were in White ceremonial uniforms, complete with Pith Helmets, which was quite a physical test for us all. One or two of the band succumbed to the heat and had to exit before they fell!

A Memorable 'Cock-up'

The next day the band was scheduled to travel into Brisbane to perform a marching display in the town centre in the late afternoon. This was going to be covered by live TV and radio under a banner such as 'The Queen's Band is in Town.' It was another hot day, around the 40-degree mark, and the band had enjoyed a free day in Brisbane with some staying onboard for 'tot' time and lunch. Big mistake!

I remember that most of the band (including me) had enjoyed a few beers during the day, but were still fine. However, two of our number had lost the plot completely and were blotto by the time we needed to change to go ashore for the marching display. We managed to get them into their ceremonial uniforms and chaperoned them ashore, undetected by the management, and onto the coach for the journey into Brisbane. One of the two was a trombone player so we stood him in the stairwell of the coach, which was the type that had 'concertina' collapsible doors. At this stage we thought we had recovered the situation and with a little more time everyone would start to sober up. Our display had been widely advertised so our arrival by bus was greeted by applause from thousands of interested spectators and rolling cameras transmitting the event around the country. As the bus came to a stop the driver opened the collapsible doors against which, by this time, the trombone player had fallen asleep! So the first pictures of our arrival was said trombone player falling out of the doors complete with trombone and collapsing in a heap, all captured nicely on film!

There was worse to come as we recovered the trombone player back into the coach (where he remained under guard) and proceeded to form up for the marching display. The Director of Music and his team were now moving amongst the remainder of us to check whether anyone else was incapable of functioning for the display. Although it was clear everyone had taken the occasional glass, it was judged that we could go ahead, and so started one of the most bizarre displays I have been involved with - and there have been a few!

Marching displays are second nature to military musicians and the rule of thumb is you follow the man in front of you. However, the drinking companion of the trombone player decided to go 'walkabout' not long after the start of the display and ended up completely detached from the rest of us, desperately trying to prove his innocence by playing his instrument as loud as possible! Others were led in various directions totally contrary to the plan and it was chaos. Quite who noticed we shall never know, but the 'walkabout' player was locked up after the display and the rest of us were given a serious bollocking on return to Britannia. John Hillier reminded me recently of the humorous postscript to this story when we returned to our mess deck onboard. The Doctor was sent for to assess whether the two worst offenders were drunk. Doc found the trombone player asleep on his bunk, still in full (filthy) white ceremonial dress holding on to his trombone with a grip like a dead man. The Doc prodded him and said, "What's the matter old son?", to which came the reply, "I want to get off this f*****g ship". The Doc just said, "It looks like it's your lucky day lad", and with that, he was gone.

The upshot of the whole debacle was that the two serious offenders were 'Dismissed Royal Yacht Service' (the ultimate sanction) and sent to Singapore to wait until Britannia arrived back in the UK before being sent home themselves. Now that's what I call a punishment!

Further visits to Townsville, Green Island on The Barrier Reef, Snapper Island, Cookstown, Cairns and finally the focal point of the tour, Botany Bay to mark Captain Cook's first landing in Australia on 28th April 1770. Another huge reception of small craft welcomed Britannia into the Bay, followed by a full-scale reenactment of Captain Cook's landing, complete with a replica ship called 'Endeavour II' and a ceremonial planting of the Union Flag on the shore. The tour ended with another few days in Sydney where The Queen was given a tremendous send-off with fireworks and the whole nine-yards for which Sydney is famous. Once the Royal Party had flown home, we poor souls began our leisurely cruise back to the UK via Pago Pago, Balboa, The Panama Canal and Bermuda, reaching Portsmouth on 15th June 1970, five years to the day I had joined the RMs. It's a tough old life!

Although this major tour was completed, there was still the normal round of events involving Britannia starting with the Tall Ships Race at the end of July, 'Cowes Week' on the Isle of Wight and the annual Western Isles cruise around Scotland to drop the Royal Party at Balmoral.

Odds and Ends

This bicentennial tour was to be the final trip for our Director of Music Captain Tom Lambert who had been furiously networking while in Australia to setup his new career 'down-under'. I had mixed feelings about Tom as a boss, from where I sat as a young man starting out and leader of his orchestra. He hadn't treated me very well in truth. I appreciated he was competent as a conductor and he had a certain charisma, but I didn't like the way he was always 'posing' and was really conducting the audience and not the band. I have seen this self-awareness in other conductors down the years but Tom was out there in front.

As with most overseas trips on ships, one person has an idea to buy a certain item and many others follow, not wanting to miss the bargain. This was the case when the NAAFI manager in Britannia had gained access to duty free watches. Word spread and many of us followed each other to buy an Omega or Rolex watch. I bought an Omega that was both waterproof and shockproof, which I tested by submerging in water and tossing across the Mess to prove its claims! Tom Lambert bought the biggest gold watch I have ever seen - it was massive. The strap was also too big which caused it to slide up and down his wrist and rattle. For a conductor a watch is a distraction and many take them off to conduct or have a discreet item which does not get in the way. Not Tom. He fancied he looked the 'real deal' with this cumbersome timepiece rattling on his arm. What a distraction for we who had to watch him. I never saw him without that watch for the rest of his time with the band. That sums Tom up for me.

Looking back on this amazing trip, it really was the first time that I got the message about the power and reach of the Royal Family and the force for good that they clearly were. A recurring theme to this day. Not only winning the hearts and minds of peoples around the world, often in the remotest of places, but also amongst world leaders who they brought together in a social setting, and encouraged people to talk to each other, especially Commonwealth leaders. Alongside this diplomacy, the business activity that Great Britain PLC was generating by association was massive, albeit difficult to quantify precisely in financial terms. All this was way beyond what politicians could hope to achieve, and often against a backdrop of our domestic media harping on about the cost of Britannia and questioning the relevance of the Royal Family. What short-sighted fools! The fact that Britannia lasted for another 26 years is a miracle, but the politicians eventually had their envy-driven way and one of our greatest national assets was scrapped and not replaced. How sad, especially as this happened the year before I took over as Director of Music of the Royal Band in 1997 - argh!

L to R: John Hillier, Wally Walters,
John Perkins, Jem Tugwood
Many a run ashore was had by this quartet!

CHAPTER 14

An early promotion opportunity by chance

It was known that the following year 1971 there was going to be a major Royal Visit to the South Pacific. It would be a five-month trip leaving in early January 1971. As leader of the orchestra I was needed for this trip, there being few decent violinists to substitute for me at that time. This meant that I may have been prevented from attending a Junior Command Course later that year at the Commando Training Centre Lympstone in order to qualify for promotion to Band Corporal. I argued a case for me to take the Junior Command Course a year early which was accepted on the basis of the priority of Royal Yacht duties so I qualified, aged 19 years, for my first promotion. In those years many musicians did not want promotion preferring to soldier on without the extra responsibilities. Bad for them but good for me! It is difficult to be sure, but I reckon this led to me being promoted (the first of eight competitive promotions throughout my service career) at least one year early aged 22 years.

We welcome a new Boss

After returning from the Captain Cook bicentennial tour of Australasia the previous year our Director of Music (Captain Tom Lambert) retired and took a job with the Australian Navy. He was replaced by a wonderful man and terrific leader who in time became the Principal Director of Music, Captain Jim Mason. Jim had served with my father in HMS Glasgow in the 1952-54 commission and used to babysit me from time to time. He said on numerous occasions that he, "Should have exterminated me at birth when he had the opportunity" - a little harsh I thought, but I was a troublesome young musician! We all liked Jim a lot. He told me recently that he joined a different Band Service, one that meant he spent 30 years of his career on ships, including Britannia. That was the life the Band Service offered his generation; so different today.

Jim was a father figure to us all, being so much older and wiser in all worldly matters. He looked every inch a Royal Marines Officer and had a quiet and subtle leadership manner which musicians responded to. He would never claim to have been a charismatic musician or conductor, neither did he produce any notable written musical compositions or arrangements, however this didn't matter to us as the band was full of good musicians who could make things happen. Jim was well liked by the Royal Family and the ship's company, which again was a plus for the band. He was a kind man too, and many have their own stories of how he helped them in one situation or another, whether this was visiting relatives when abroad or compassionate reasons for getting back to family. He knew how to surround himself with strong musicians who could produce exceptional results that in turn reflected well on him. I kept in touch with Jim and Alice (RIP) down the years and we even spent Christmas with them and their daughter Linda and Colin Priestland (a Naval dentist) while serving with Colin in HMS Raleigh in the mid-80s. At the time of writing this Jim is in his 90th year and as sharp as ever. Jim and I were to serve together happily both in Britannia and later in The RMSM Deal between 1978-82 when Jim was the Principal Director of Music and I was his Warrant Officer (Bandmaster).

Jim's first significant trip in Britannia started on 15th January 1971 when Britannia left Portsmouth for the start of a major five-month deployment. The passage across the Atlantic Ocean included stops at Madeira and Barbados to refuel, before sailing through the Panama Canal and berthing in Balboa. Over the next days the Royal Party joined Britannia. The Royal Party included, Prince Philip, Princess Alexandra, Lord Mountbatten together with Lord and Lady Brabourne (later Countess Mountbatten), Sir Solly Zuckerman, and the Hon. Angus Ogilvy. On 5th February we set sail for the Galapagos Islands.

Some of the band enjoying deck sports
Back L to R: Malc Thompson (RIP), Lyn 'Jamie' James, Tony
Oliver, John Perkins
Middle: Charlie Fleming, *Front:* A member of the RM detachment

CHAPTER 15

A wonderful trip to the South Pacific Islands, the USA and Canada (1971)

Lord Louis Mountbatten knew my Father!

Shortly after joining Britannia Lord Louis Mountbatten asked to meet all the Royal Marines onboard in the Recreation Space. Lord Louis was the Colonel Commandant of the Royal Marines, a position he was very proud of. He started by asking the assembled group how many Royal Marines were onboard. Someone answered 35, to which he answered no, 36, never forget I too am a Royal Marine!

Lord Louis and Princess Anne in Britannia
© *Crown copyright*

He then went on to relate one his favourite stories about a concert in Malta in 1953 given in Sliema Hall by the massed bands of the Mediterranean Fleet. Lord Louis was Commander of the Mediterranean Fleet at the time in the Flagship HMS Glasgow. He informed us that after the concert rehearsals the bands returned to their ships for a meal before returning to the concert venue for the performance. Minutes before the musicians went on stage the principal cornet player opened his case to find his barbering equipment neatly stored inside. The barbering case being identical to his cornet case! Lord Louis said (with a smile) this particular musician was well known in the ship as a great character who was either cutting hair, taking pictures, or working other less formal rackets. I sheepishly put my hand up and said, "Sir, that is my father you are describing". My father had told me this story many times before. Lord Louis couldn't have been happier to have his story verified. Not only that, but our new Director of Music Jim Mason was a Band Sergeant in the same HMS Glasgow Band with my father and could offer further verification. I spoke with Jim recently to confirm these details, which he remembers clearly. Small world!

The Galapagos Islands

In 1971 the Galapagos Islands[16] was not a tourist destination as it is today, and it was a rare privilege to get to see this unique habitat. The Royal party spent most of the days ashore

---

[16] Our second visit in three years to these Islands.

exploring the frigate birds, red-footed boobies, masked boobies, land iguanas, marine iguanas, sea lions and, most famously, giant tortoises. We were given the same unrestricted access to explore at will with them. Other than scientists and a very few locals, we were the only people on the islands. All these species had developed in the Galapagos independent of mankind, and they had no fear whatsoever of humans. It was possible to walk amongst them and not cause the slightest concern of any danger. From what I am told, today there are many more restrictions as tourists flock to the islands (at great expense) to see what we witnessed for free, and without restriction. I told you it was a good job!

The Galapagos Islands
Lord Louis, Princess Alexandra & Lady Brabourne
13th February 1971
© *Crown copyright*

After a few days in Galapagos we set sail for the 6-day cruise to Easter Island. These sea-days were relaxing times for us as we were not especially busy during the daytime and, other than playing background music for dinners and the occasional concert, we had lots of free time. The most memorable event during this passage was the 'Crossing the Line' ceremony, the traditional 'nod' to King Neptune when crossing the Equator. Lord Mountbatten, Princess Alexandra, the Brabournes and others of the Royal Household were hauled before King Neptune, before being tipped into the tank of water and dunked by the 'bears'. Us mere mortals, who had not crossed the line before followed close behind. Other activities at sea included 'Horse Racing' on the foc'sle, Deck Tennis (at which I was Yacht Champion for two years) and other deck games, quizzes, curry nights and so on[17]. Add a few beers to any of the above and life was very enjoyable.

Easter Island

Finally, after 1962 kilometres and six days steaming across the Pacific, we arrived at Easter Island, and so began another unique adventure in this remote spot in the middle of the Pacific. Easter Island is a Chilean island in the southeastern Pacific Ocean. The Island is most famous for its nearly 1000 monumental stone statues, called *Moai*. In 1995, UNESCO named Easter

---

[17] I was also Yacht Chess Champion for two years, being eventually beaten by Commander 'Dicky' Bird in the final of year three.

Charlie Fleming and John doing their bit in the Tug-of-War competition on the foc'sle

Island a World Heritage Site, with much of the island protected within Rapa Nui National Park. Easter Island is one of the most remote inhabited islands in the world. The nearest inhabited land is Pitcairn Island, 2,075 kilometres away and the nearest continental point lies in Chile, 3,512 kilometres away.

A few of us hired horses to explore further, although I did feel guilty riding a horse that was so undernourished and thin. We visited the large volcanic crater and various burial sites where the origins of the many stone figures, found all over the island, are the subject of much debate. These stone figures, called *Moai*, are monolithic human figures carved by the Rapa Nui people on Easter Island between the years 1250 and 1500. Nearly half are still at Rano Raraku, the main *Moai* quarry, but hundreds were transported from there and set on stone platforms called ahu around the island's perimeter. Almost all *Moai* have overly large heads three-eighths the size of the whole statue. The production and transportation of the almost 1000 statues is considered a remarkable creative and physical feat. The tallest *Moai* erected, called *Paro*, was almost 10 metres (33ft) high and weighed 82 tonnes. The heaviest *Moai* erected was a shorter but squatter *Moai* at Ahu Tongariki, weighing 86 tonnes. One unfinished sculpture, if completed, would have been approximately 21m (69ft) tall, with a weight of about 145-165 tons. The *Moai* were toppled in the late 18th and early 19th centuries, possibly as a result of European contact or internecine tribal wars.

Verification by King Neptune of my 'Crossing The Line'.

The Island has very little vegetation to sustain its many wild horses and small population, so there was a sense that the best times were behind them. Very different from its past when the land was heavily forested and fertile. From Easter Island the Yacht headed west to Pitcairn Island.

Pitcairn Island

The remote island of Pitcairn was uninhabited until the 18th century when it became a safe haven for Fletcher Christian and his band of mutineers from HMS Bounty. Having cast the Commanding Officer, William Bligh, and eighteen other men adrift in one of the ship's boats the mutineers set sail for Tahiti, where some decided to stay. The remaining mutineers were joined by several Tahitians for the voyage to Pitcairn Island. Despite the odds, Bligh and his men managed to make an epic voyage of 3600 miles in the open boat to reach the island of Timor[18]. When Bligh returned to Great Britain and informed the Admiralty of the mutiny they dispatched HMS Pandora to Tahiti to bring the mutineers back to stand trial. Of the ten who were brought back three were hung for their part in the mutiny. As for those who chose the relative safety of Pitcairn Island they were faced with the prospect of creating a sustainable community on an Island just two miles long and one mile wide which rises to over 1000 feet. However, 182 years later the island was supporting a community of 92 people, most of whom were direct descendants of the original mutineers.

Shortly after anchoring at Pitcairn Island two motor launches were sent to the small harbour to collect 50 islanders to take tea onboard and listen to a concert by our band. A more different world it is hard to imagine from the life of an islander on Pitcairn. The following day the Royal Party made the tricky landing via launches and transferring to the islanders' long boats in order to negotiate the surf into the small landing area. Soon afterwards the band made the same crossing complete with all the band equipment required to perform a marching display somewhere on the island. As our Director of Music Jim Mason recalls in The Official History of the Royal Yacht, "I explained to the Island's Secretary, Ben Christian that I wanted to perform a Beating Retreat (marching display), but the problem was that I needed a flat space to do it on. He told me that I should use their village square. I asked him where it was and he told me that I was standing in it. It was exactly 7 yards by 3 yards which was tight for 26 of us marching up and down, but we had to do it." (adapt and overcome).

Pitcairn appeared to me a tropical paradise, the stuff of 'Swiss Family Robinson', requiring a special mindset to live a life there without contact with the outside world, yet this is what the mutineers did. Conflicts between individuals flared up inevitably and the number of males reduced over the years, but survive as a community they did. Pitcairn was a fascinating place that we had the privilege to see firsthand thanks to Britannia.

---

[18] Timor is an island at the southern end of Maritime Southeast Asia, north of the Timor Sea.

The Cook Islands

It was another emotional farewell at Pitcairn with the islanders singing their traditional tunes of 'Cling to the Bible My Boy' and 'The Sinking of the Vestris' interspersed with ourselves playing our traditional songs on the Royal Deck as was the custom on leaving harbour in every port. Our new destination was the Cook Islands, a five-day voyage away and an opportunity for everyone to enjoy life at sea in the South Pacific. All manner of activities came back into play, with tug-of-war, crazy sports, quick dressing competitions, deck sports and a nightly inter-mess quiz. On the morning of 27th February, the Yacht reached her next destination of Raratonga, the most populous of the Cook Islands, for a whistle-stop visit before heading on to Palmerston Island. Palmerston Island is a coral atoll in the Cook Islands northwest of Rarotonga. It was discovered by James Cook in 1774. In 1863 William Marsters, a ship's carpenter and barrel maker, arrived on Palmerston from Manuae with two Polynesian wives. He added a third wife and sired a large family of some 23 children, whose descendants now inhabit Palmerston. Thus, Palmerston Island is the only island in the Cook Islands for which English is the native language. Palmerston came under New Zealand administration in 1901.

Palmerston was an unscheduled visit as the Yacht was en route to our next formal destination of Samoa. As Countess Mountbatten explains in 'The Official History' of Britannia, "We were very taken aback because we were due to go ashore at 3pm so we thought that we would eat lunch on board and only be offered tea ashore. When we got ashore a table had been laid along the village street. This table was laden with food including their version of Cornish pasties. We had to do our best to eat this banquet on top of our lunch!" The Royal Party was hosted by Ned Masters, a direct descendant of William Masters. How impressive would it have been for the locals to see Britannia cruising into their waters with all the pomp and ceremony associated with a Royal visit. The stuff of folklore.

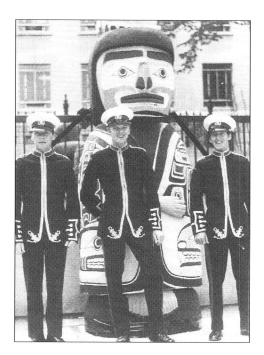

L to R: Tony Oliver, John Hillier & John Perkins ashore in Esquimalt Canada 1971

CHAPTER 16

Samoa

The evening before entering harbour at Samoa, the Royal Party gathered on the foc'sle with members of the ship's company for a concert by our band, including all the favourites from military music to Big Band music and show tunes. The highlight of our show was a performance of the Post Horn Galop performed by Charlie Soloman our Principal Cornet player. As Prince Philip recalls, "The Marine Bandsman appeared as a plumber with tools and a urinal in his bag. He took it out and fitted a piece of flexible hose to the outlet end and then put a bugle mouthpiece in the other end of the hose. No one was quite certain what he was doing at the time. He then proceeded to play 'Post Horn Galop' on this curious instrument!"

Charlie Soloman working his
magic with the urinal!

The next morning Britannia weighed anchor for Samoa. Samoa, officially the Independent State of Samoa and, until 1997, known as Western Samoa, is a country consisting of two main islands, Savai'i and Upolu, and four smaller islands, Manono, Apolima, Fanuatapu, and Namua. The capital city is Apia. The Lapita people discovered and settled the Samoan Islands around 3,500 years ago. They developed a unique Samoan language and Samoan cultural identity. The country is a member of the Commonwealth of Nations, and Western Samoa was admitted to the United Nations in 1976. The entire island group, which includes American Samoa, was called 'Navigator Islands' by European explorers before the 20th century because of the Samoans' seafaring skills. The country was governed by New Zealand until its independence in 1962.

Entering harbour routine was enacted with all the flags and ceremonial together with the RM Band playing a selection of tunes from the Royal Deck. It is worth mentioning that another small idiosyncrasy of Britannia's traditions is that no verbal orders/commands were to be given above decks. This allowed for a serene atmosphere and impression of slick professionalism, which was indeed the case. So in place of verbal orders a series of hand signals took their place which applied to all activities including the band drills for making ready to play or rest, and every other specialisation onboard. It was so well rehearsed that it struck the observer as a 'well-oiled machine' - which was the intention. On this occasion Britannia was escorted into Apia by the long 'fautasi' boats each powered by 50 Samoan oarsmen. Quite a sight.

Following the usual round of official engagements throughout the day the Royal Party stayed ashore in the house once occupied by Robert Louis Stevenson. The second full day was largely dominated by various local sports during which we (the Band) would provide musical entertainments at suitable 'dull' moments. Sadly it was rainy and the sports area, being grass and mud, became very waterlogged and brought back memories of the many agricultural shows bands play for back in the UK. When the ground is too wet for the cattle they send on the band! Spot the difference I hear you say!

That same evening we were quickly back onboard and cleaning up ready to play as a small orchestra for the formal dinner in honour of His Highness Malietoa Tanumafili II and the Samoan Cabinet. This was a typical day's work for the band on most all these Island visits. And so onwards to Fiji.

Fiji

Luckily I still have some 'super 8' movie film of the Fiji visit which, although poor quality, brings back the Polynesian colour and excitement of the Royal visit. The first port of call into Lakeba was dogged by stormy weather which delayed the Royal programme for a few hours. Once the Royal Barge was away the Royal Party had to transfer to local canoes for the final approach to the beach at which point the canoe was carried ashore by 20 strong men and placed on the grass to avoid their guests getting wet feet! After a day of formal engagements Britannia left Lakeba to the sound of 'Isa Lei' sung by thousands of well-wishers on the beach; another magical moment.

The next day we arrived in Kadavu (the fourth largest island in Fiji) where the band was scheduled to perform a concert ashore for the ladies of the Island. We had a tricky passage ashore having to transfer from Britannia's boats into canoes for the final few hundred yards, before disembarking in the sea carrying all our musical equipment above our heads (adapt and overcome). The day became more memorable as our Director of Music Jim Mason explains, "They put out some chairs for us and we were about ready to start when the head lady turned to me and said, "Before you start we would like you to drink Kava". I had drunk it before so knew what to expect. There is a set routine as to how one is expected to drink it so I turned to the young men in the band and said, "Do exactly what I do and whatever happens drink it, no matter what the taste!" Kava is always brought by a young girl who brings the drink in a half coconut and kneels down to offer up the drink. You then have to clap your hands three times, pick up the kava, drink it straight down, hand the coconut back, and clap your hands three times again, then off she goes. Kava tastes a bit like soapy water with a slight minty taste. The Band all drank their Kava and we played the first number. I was about to start the second number when this lady said she would like us to drink Kava again. Every time we stopped we went through this same routine again. After this had happened a few of times I turned to the lady and said that if this was alcoholic we couldn't keep going. She said it wasn't, but the ladies would be offended if we didn't drink Kava so thereafter we just kept going. While Kava isn't alcoholic, it is a paralysing drug which anaesthetises the tongue. After about half an hour we couldn't play anymore because of the effects of the Kava that we had been given, so we were taken on a tour of the island instead!"

From Kadavu it was to Lautoka, the second largest city in Fiji after the capital Suva, before leaving the Fiji Islands on 17th March for the Solomon Islands.

The Solomon Islands

The Solomon Islands consist of six major islands and over 900 smaller islands in Oceania lying to the east of Papua New Guinea. The country's capital, Honiara, is located on the island of Guadalcanal. The country takes its name from the Solomon Islands archipelago, which is a collection of Melanesian Islands that also includes the North Solomon Islands, part of Papua New Guinea. With the outbreak of the Second World War most planters and traders were evacuated to Australia and most cultivation ceased. Some of the most intense fighting during the war occurred in the Solomons. The most significant of the Allied Forces' operations against the Japanese Imperial Forces was launched on 7th August 1942, with simultaneous naval bombardments and amphibious landings on the Florida Islands at Tulagi and Red Beach on Guadalcanal. The Battle of Guadalcanal became an important and bloody campaign fought in the Pacific War as the Allies began to repulse the Japanese expansion. Of strategic importance during the war were the coast-watchers operating in remote locations, often on Japanese held islands. These coast-watchers provided early warning and intelligence of Japanese naval, army and aircraft movements during the campaign.

Our visit coincided with a time of discovery in the islands of large deposits of copper and gold high in the hills. Vast sums of money had been invested in a new port and homes for the workers required to work the mines. The transformation of this tropical paradise into the industrial age was the main story when we were there. It would be interesting to go there again and see if they managed to disguise the mining activities and retain the natural landscape. We had so far travelled almost 10,000 miles across the Pacific Ocean and were closing fast on Madang - New Guinea.

Guadalcanal 1971

CHAPTER 17

Madang - New Guinea

I am certain Madang is more developed today than it was 50 years ago, but when we arrived we were left in no doubt by briefings onboard that kidnap, cannibalism and all sorts of tricky business was still rife in New Guinea. To be sure it did seem a very basic place carved out of the jungle, but what an atmosphere. Vast crowds from all parts of New Guinea came to welcome the Royal Party. Apparently some had walked for weeks through the jungles to be there to witness the arrival of Prince Philip and his party. Singers, dancers, together with highly decorated boats made for a spectacle not to be forgotten.

One evening we took some instruments ashore to play a 5-piece dance band in a local bar. I was on trumpet because the more able trumpet players didn't want the 'gig'! Needless to say we had a great time and we were plied with beers for the whole evening. During the course of the evening I spoke with an English couple who were living in Madang as part of the consulate staff. At the end of the evening they insisted that we all go back to their house for a nightcap (normally a bad idea!) so we piled into the transport they had hastily arranged. This impromptu party headed deep into the 'bush' towards their jungle type house where we were surrounded by the sounds of the tropical forest at night, without a clue as to how we would get back to Britannia. Anyway, after an evening of free beer we were up for anything, but what we found on entering the house was the most civilised of dwellings and an abundance of food and drink which was most welcome. Once we had eaten our host asked me what music I liked to which I replied 'classical', not expecting for one moment that any such music might exist in New Guinea, let alone the forest beyond Madang. To my delight, a box set of Handel's 'Messiah'

appeared as if by magic and we started to listen to these old 78rpm recordings of one of classical music's most iconic pieces. The combination of the jungle setting, the boozy evening and the genial company was truly magical and the perfect end to a really special visit.

Impromptu Dance Band in the Rec. Space
Bill Williamson (Sax) John Hillier (Sax) Me (on trumpet) Tony Oliver (Trom) Wally Hibbert (piano) Jack Kennedy (bass)
Ronnie Ellam (drums)

The next morning we were due to leave Madang when I got a message to go to the gangway as I had a visitor. To my surprise there was mine host from the previous evening with the box set of The Messiah in his hands. He insisted that I take the recordings as a gift and he wouldn't take no for an answer. After thanking him profusely for the gift and the hospitality the previous night we said our goodbyes. I kept those recordings for over 40 years, never playing them, but storing them in one loft after another as we moved from house to house. I eventually passed them on to someone who had a 78rpm player! Hallelujah!

Madang marked the end of this early part of the trip as the Royal Party left on 22nd March to fly back to the UK. Britannia started the long voyage north via Pearl Harbour, San Francisco and Esquimalt (Victoria, Canada) to arrive in Vancouver on 30th April ready for the embarkation of The Queen, Prince Philip and Princess Anne on 3rd May, for the start of their tour of Western Canada.

Having so much time between Royal Duties made for a leisurely cruise north with lengthy stays in both Pearl Harbour, Hawaii and San Francisco. I remember one of the first nights in Pearl Harbour going to the Naval Club where a 'Bluegrass' band was playing. In amongst the band was an amazing violinist who was playing with jaw-dropping skills yet still fitting in with the 'Bluegrass' style. I could do nothing other than sit and listen, totally captivated by what I was hearing. When the band had a break I went across and introduced myself as being 'Leader of the Orchestra in HMY Britannia' which seemed to catch his attention. I said I was totally impressed with his playing, the like of which I had never heard before in a Bluegrass band, and asked him where he learnt to play like that. It turned out that he too was a classical violinist who played Bluegrass for fun, his primary job being Professor of Violin at the Hawaii Conservatory of Music!

This chance encounter gave me an idea to write ahead to the Victoria (Canada) Conservatory of Music to ask whether I could pay a visit to the Conservatory when we were in Victoria a few weeks later. Not only was this agreed, but I was taken under the wing of one of the violin professors who provided some tickets to a concert he was playing in and also gave me a couple of lessons on unaccompanied Bach. Result!

It's not my fault

From time to time events occur that are neither planned nor preventable. One such occasion was in Esquimalt Victoria where a group of us went ashore for a look around during a free afternoon. On leaving the Yacht in uniform we met a family who noticed our band uniform and introduced themselves as old friends of our Director of Music Jim Mason. In fact the man had been a trombone player (sorry forgotten his name) in the Band Service many years before when he had served with Jim. This very friendly and generous couple insisted that we accompany them to a party they were having to mark the visit of Britannia. They had hoped to meet Jim and take him to the party, but he was unavailable and they appeared really pleased to have our little group of about five musicians as a substitute. And so began an afternoon of socialising in the company of our newly discovered friends.

Sometimes, try as you might, especially as a 20-year-old, events take over and good judgement goes out of the window. This particular afternoon fitted perfectly in that category. In the midst of our excitement, being made to feel so important by our hosts, we had rather lost track of time, so it was in a bit of a panic that someone realised we needed to get back to Britannia to play for the Royal Dinner onboard that evening. To make matters worse we were anchored off shore and had to wait for the boat routines to get back to Britannia. Luckily, we did manage to get a boat and returned just in time to grab a shower to sober up and change to go and play for the dinner.

Sometime during this transition I realised that I was the only one of us five revellers playing in the orchestra for the dinner, the others played instruments that were not required for the small orchestra. Not only that, but I was Leader of the Orchestra as principal violinist and the music programme was littered with violin solos. I remember this included the overture 'Orpheus in the Underworld' by Offenbach (includes the famous tricky violin solo) and 'Shortcake Walk' by Sydney Torch, which starts with a solo violin. This did not end well! In truth I couldn't read the music clearly and I was playing mostly by memory. I would have hoped that one of the other violinists jumped in with the solos, but no - cheers! Playing the violin when having consumed too much alcohol does not work, unlike a brass instrument which (for many others) was less of a problem. Although I got through the dinner, it was not my finest hour, which was made very clear by Jim Mason the next day. In one afternoon, I had undone all the good work that I had been doing - my self-destruct button was working well!

It was a lesson learned the hard way about the perils of partying before working. A constant trade-off for all musicians whose lifestyles constantly come into conflict between the two. We were only substituting for the Director of Music with his old friend. They say 'no good deed goes unpunished'!

Vancouver

Vancouver was the main focal point of this mini Royal Tour of British Columbia (BC), although lots of the formal events took place in the capital Victoria. Vancouver has the most amazing natural backdrop of the Rocky Mountains, which were covered with snow when we were there. It is a gorgeous place for the visitor with so much to see. I was struck how the residents seem to identify more with the state of BC than Canada as a whole. It is a vast country and BC is in the extreme West so I suppose it is understandable. We had a lot of free time during this stay as the Canadians wanted to provide all the music for formal events which freed us up to enjoy the sights.

After the Royal Visit to Vancouver came to an end, the band was required to fly back to the UK to be in position to join the massed bands of the Royal Marines at the Royal Tournament in Earls Court Exhibition Centre London. The earliest flight we could get with the RAF was about seven days after Britannia sailed, so we moved into hotel accommodation to wait out this period. Tough old life! When we were due to fly we made our way to the airport with our instruments and uniforms needed for the Royal Tournament to discover our transport was an old propeller troop carrier plane, the type that was designed for short-hop flights. The RAF were using this flight as a training flight for newbie pilots to chalk up some flying hours. The pilot in charge greeted us with the news that there was no ground crew so could we crack on and load the plane. So began a long haul flight from Western Canada, stopping only at Gander (Eastern Canada) to refuel. Hardly the modern jets we take for granted today. Anyway it was a reminder of the highs and lows of Service life that is part and parcel of the job.

Canada was the start of a love affair with golf that has so far lasted almost 50 years. It all started by chance towards the end of this tour.

The Royal Yacht Ship's Company 1970

CHAPTER 18

Strange things Happen on Golf Courses

The Patterson Golf Trophy 1985
Cay being presented with the winners cup by John.
Cay has always been the better golfer!

My first experience on the golf course was at the end of the tour to British Columbia. Western Canada boasts the most stunning countryside, equal to anything in the world. As with most tours in Britannia, the Ship's Company received numerous invitations to go to a variety of local attractions, all free of charge. Myself and another life-long friend, trombonist Tony Oliver, decided to give golf a go. Tony was a very good natural sportsman and a central member of Britannia's football team. I was competitive at most sports, especially squash, badminton and deck tennis[19]. The golf clubs were being supplied by the host club as part of the invitation so we set off to do our best. I remember clearly being smitten by the game and all that goes with it, from the etiquette to the beautiful surroundings that are part and parcel of golf course estates. I think we made a reasonable fist of our first outing on the course and were helped in large part by our hosts who realised we were two young lads new to golf. The golf was followed by a nice meal and a few drinks together with conversation and the chance to learn something extra about the country. That is the attraction of golf, right there.

When we returned to the UK a few weeks later to join the massed bands at the Royal Tournament we already had the golf bug and took every opportunity to get out and play. Fortunately the Royal Navy/Marines had concessions to a number of courses in Hampshire, including beautiful courses such as Liphook, Hindhead and Hayling Island. We were out there come rain or shine and would often play 36 holes in the same day, starting in the rain, and, more than once, in light snow! We quickly reduced our handicaps down to around 12, where mine has remained for 45 years without much change. Tony became better than this and his sons better still in low single figures. My sons are natural golfers and would be low handicap players if

---

[19] A game for two or four players, designed for the limited space aboard ship and also played as a garden game. A rubber ring, or quoit, is thrown across a net. It must be caught using one hand and returned immediately with the same hand from the point of catch. I was a regular winner at this game for some unknown reason!

they ever joined a club! The one thing that did change is that I became a 'fair-weather' golfer, and the days of deliberately playing in bad weather are long gone.

As the golf commentator Henry Longhurst said, "Golf certainly takes you to some beautiful places" and throughout my time in Britannia I played in beautiful places whenever we had invites. In January 1972 we set sail on an extended Royal Tour of the Far East. Our first refuelling stop was the Portuguese Island of Madeira off the North West African coast. For us single men this first stop in the sunshine was a great feeling so when we eventually finished our Beating Retreat rehearsal for the ship's Cocktail Party we went ashore to check out the night life. The capital of Madeira is Funchal, a beautiful old fishing port with colourful boats (bum boats) and a horseshoe shaped bay with hills rising up to the mountains which surround the port. Very beautiful at night with all the house lights shining brightly almost like a fireworks display. I had already signed up to play golf at the only course on the Island (there is now more than one course) up in the hills on the mountainside. Predictably we all had some heavy-duty hangovers after the night before and left for the golf course in the transport wishing we hadn't agreed to play. My round started bad and rapidly got worse. I even had a 10 on the par 5, 7th hole. However the 8th hole was a blind-shot hole over the brow of a hill down to the par 3 green. I hit a 5-iron and hoped for the best. On arrival at the green we found my ball in the hole; hole-in-one! My success was short-lived as on the next hole I scored 8. So my card read 10- 1 - 8. The rest of the card was as bad. Great celebrations were had afterwards at my expense!

Life Stranger Than Fiction

They say that life is stranger than fiction, and so it proved two years later. We had sailed again in early January for another Royal Tour and stopped for refuelling in Madeira. Golf was arranged again and we set off in routine fashion with much banter on the transport about the last time we played and my hole-in-one. 'Let's see whether you can do it again' etc….. I think my reply was along the lines of "yes, this shouldn't be a problem." On arrival we were allocated Caddies (local lads who were in truth better golfers than us) who were to advise us on the perils of the course and give advice generally. When my turn came to tee off on the 1st hole - a 215-yard par 3 hole - I took out a 3-wood club hoping this might do the job. However, my caddie became very agitated and insisted (in Portuguese) that I take a 5-wood club as this was better for the distance. I doubt I had ever taken a 5-wood club off the tee, but I gave way to his advice and hit the 5-wood. As if by magic, the ball sailed high in the air straight for the green. The players in front of us had just put the flag back in the hole when my ball landed on the green and rolled gently up to the hole and dropped in!!! A hole-in-one, again![20]

---

[20] I have since had another hole-in-one in Portsmouth and Cay has had a hole-in-one at Walmer and Kingsdown golf club (11th hole) just outside Deal in Kent.

So having played the course only twice, each time I had managed a hole-in-one. Surely some sort of record? My wife Cay and I have had a number of holidays in Madeira, yet I dare not play the golf course again lest I spoil my 100% record!

Another memorable round of golf took place in Singapore a year later. An invitation for two golfers to play at Royal Singapore Golf Club was placed on the ship's noticeboard. Interested parties would usually add their names to the list, but for some odd reason nobody had taken this offer. It turned out that all the usual golfing suspects were busy with duties or other things, so I added my name, as did another member of the band (who shall remain nameless) who was not known as a golfer, but said he would like to 'have a go'. We were picked up by courtesy car and taken to the club where we were met by the Club Captain and the Club Champion Golfer. Coming from the Royal Yacht it was very usual to be treated like royalty (in the absence of the real thing) and so we were wined and dined and pressed for information about the life we led in Britannia. After a highly enjoyable lunch (being made to feel very important) we changed and made our way to the 1st Tee, complete with caddies whom the club also supplied.

It is worth pointing out at this stage that I had been playing golf for a couple of years by now and I imagine my handicap would have been a respectable 12 or so. However, my (nameless) playing partner was a complete beginner, and, although we had carried off the lunch, drinks and conversation with a respectable level of competence, this was now crunch time. We were invited to tee-off first. I hit an average drive that was neither good nor bad. My playing partner took an almighty swing at his ball and missed it completely, starting a tally of 'air' shots[21] that became the predominant theme of his round of golf. I remember him making contact with the ball at the second attempt causing the ball to make a spectacular swerve to the right and disappear 'out-of-bounds' towards the car park. To their eternal credit our two hosts (who were both superb golfers) quickly summed up the situation realising we were young lads who just wanted to get ashore for a change of scenery. They made light of our low-standard golf and tried to give us a masterclass as we went around, with variable success. The most memorable point of the round was a 'blind hole' (much like my first hole-in-one in Madeira) where the caddies went ahead to the brow of the hill to spot where the balls landed (hopefully) further down the fairway. Our hosts teed off first as they won every hole (!), and I followed. So far so good. My playing partner followed with his trademark huge swing, this time catching the ball at the first attempt. The ball left his club and travelled like an arrow with pin-point accuracy towards his caddy standing 100 yards or so down the fairway. The ball hit the caddy in the small of his back and he dropped like a stone where he remained motionless for a few seconds, during which time a headline of 'Royal golfers kill a harmless caddy during Queen's visit' ran through my head. However our wonderful caddy, the poor lad, got to his feet and ran back towards us

---

[21] When a genuine attempt to hit the ball makes no connection with the ball, but counts as a shot nonetheless.

apologising for getting in the way of my partners ball. A humbling experience all round, and a fitting end to a fairly disastrous day where we had been 'punching above our weight' from start to finish. Another little lesson learned!

1972 Hole in One Card
Note the 10-1-8 sequence!

1974 Hole in One Card
An 'Ace' on the first hole!

CHAPTER 19

Military Training

My generation joined The Royal Marines Band Service with no expectation of using weapons in peacetime and limited expectation of military training. Military musicians had traditionally acted as medical orderlies during times of war, and in the case of RM musicians (such as my father) they were mostly serving in RN ships where their main task was to work in the Transmitting Station (TS) low down in the ship, hence the huge number of casualties taken by the Band Service during the Second World War. Training took the form of 'Transition to War' training and on-the-job training. In fact during the three years plus training at the RM School of Music there was no element of military training or weapons training. So it was with a large slice of shock and horror that all ranks were confronted with a new initiative of a 2-week package of military training starting in late 1969. This included weapons training with SLR Rifles, map reading, setting up Observation Posts (OPs), and other military tasks. And so started a battle of wills that lasted for many years - certainly throughout my whole career.

I have always hated wasting time and more importantly asking others to waste theirs. Equally I have had huge respect for fellow musicians, recognising their talent and hard work. For many years some military trainers had no conception of the level of dedication and skill that was required to be a professional musician and simply saw The Band Service as yet another group of recruits who needed to learn all the skills they might teach Commando recruits[22]. In the worst cases it was seen as 'Bandy Bashing' by the occasional mindless Platoon Weapons (PW) instructor. It didn't work well treating experienced musicians and buglers of all ranks and ages this way. To repeat the experience year-on-year was an even greater insult to the Band Service, when other military personnel serving in the same establishment did nothing of the sort. The whole procedure was a negative factor for recruitment and retention and, because of this, we lost a number of good musicians who were not prepared to undergo this annual ritual well into their middle age.

In the early days musicians took much pleasure in stripping the rifles down and deliberately letting the springs fly everywhere, much to the annoyance of the instructors. Deliberately obstructing the process became the only rewarding part of the whole experience but, for all its irritating predictability, it did provide humorous moments. Down the years we all became used to these weeks, and occasionally we were allocated instructors who were more in-tune with who they were teaching and made it more palatable while at the same time as getting across their

---

[22] I have always had the greatest respect for Commandos and their professional military skills: they are second to none.

message. Unfortunately, during my service, this was the exception to the rule. An annual personal weapons test (APWT) & Nuclear, Biological, and Chemical weapons test (NBC) would have been sufficient in peacetime - 2 days max. As my old friend (Captain) John Hillier used to say, "Every time I put on all the military training garb, I turn into a blithering idiot." I know the feeling. Annual Military Training ran for the last 30 years of my 35-year career, so if you managed to catch them all that equated to around one year of your life!

A few memorable moments

In 1985 I was The Director of Music of the Band of HM Royal Marines, Flag Officer Plymouth when the Band was tasked to take part in a National Defence exercise called exercise 'Brave Defender'. We were sent to a remote location near the Scottish Border called 'Spadeadam' a redundant military asset in the middle of nowhere. The whole area was under the command of Major Bob Bruce whom I had known from my Officer Training at the Commando Training Centre at Lympstone in Devon. Bob Bruce was a good man who knew the Band Service well. He allowed us to go about our business and setup the whole site with defensive positions, cooking facilities, stores facilities and tents for accommodation. By the mid 1980s bands were proficient at all these activities, and what we didn't know we could work out. After about a week in this location The Major General in command of this exercise flew in by helicopter with the Principal Director of Music for a 'morale boosting' visit.

I was tasked to meet them and show them around the site and our setup. Around the perimeters we had established Observation Posts (OPs) with two men lying in a concealed position covering an 'arc of fire' that would overlap both left and right of their positions with other OPs to complete a 360 degrees defensive circle. On arriving at the first OP we saw two musicians prostrate on the ground 'looking the part' with their rifles in the ready position in front of them. All suitably impressive, until The General went alongside the first musician, Musician Eddy Gasser, and noticed he was not attached to his weapon, which was propped on a sandbag, but he was writing in a notebook. The General inquired, "What are you writing soldier?", to which Eddy replied, "Poetry, Sir, would you like to hear it?" I cannot remember what came next, but I think the General was smart enough to recognise what he was seeing. This really summed up the pretence that was going on with 'round pegs' in 'square holes', a little like the Private Pike in TV comedy 'Dad's Army'. I should point out that Eddy Gasser was a superb all-round musician with a specialty as a top-quality trombone player. His wife Carol was a former Saxophone player in the renowned Ivy Benson Big Band. Eddy, a gentle man in every way, should not have been employed lying in a hole in the ground (at almost 40 years old) on the Scottish border, certainly not in peacetime.

Another time when serving at the RMSM Deal we were given a map march across country towards a destination en route to Canterbury. Having been briefed on our objective, which was basically to get to the destination, we set off in small groups. My group didn't really have the appetite for a long walk, so on leaving Deal we hopped on the Canterbury bus and got off at the Red Lion pub in Wingham where we had a few pints before walking the mile or so left in the exercise. It ended a jolly day out really, but it was basically a waste of time.

Command Courses

However, Command Courses represented good value and were useful both for gaining knowledge and leadership training which is transferable into any career, military or civilian - they had purpose. There were three levels of Command Course: Junior, Senior and Advanced. There were similarities in all, each lasting about 6 to 8 weeks. Subjects included some military skills, including weapons, map reading, tactics and planning, giving orders (in the military format) and giving and receiving lectures. All this was confidence building and relevant to future employments. They all took place at the Commando Training Centre (CTCRM) at Lympstone in Devon, where I would one day become the Director of Music.

Senior Command Course Band 1/74 - John third from right back row

I had a high regard for CTCRM which was a professional place geared to training new entrant Commandos to the Royal Marines and promotion courses. Needless to say it was a place that maintained tough standards across the board, and I always felt the calibre of the military trainers at CTCRM was much higher than those seconded to the Band Service.

I learned a lot of useful information during these courses and learned a good deal about my strengths and weaknesses during the process. I didn't excel on the command courses (I only took the Junior and Senior Command Courses before Special Duties (SD) Officer Course), but I did OK and, as we were all contemporaries, we had a good laugh in the process. It is interesting to see how the civilian world has adopted many of these leadership techniques in the intervening years. Why not? Good leadership has many universal truths. Civilian or military.

CHAPTER 20

What Else Was Happening?

In between all these glamorous Royal Tours and leadership training, life was full of the bread and butter work that made up the bulk of our daily life. Concerts around the country in all the great halls from London to Wales and Scotland. Parades and National Ceremonial events such as Beating Retreat on Horseguards Parade, Royal Tournaments, Edinburgh Tattoos and International events along the same lines.

I also played for all the Royal Weddings up to the year 2000, culminating in being the Director of Music of the Royal Band for the wedding of Prince Edward and Sophie Rhys-Jones in St George's Chapel Windsor on 19th June 1999 (*see Appendix Three*). I was lucky enough to be in Britannia for the honeymoon of Princess Anne and Mark Philips in the early 1970s. It all seemed very normal to us. There were many occasions when we were playing for political leaders and visiting Heads of State, quite often for dinners and receptions, which were more interesting as they were up close and personal.

Alongside this was music on the lighter side such as dances, cocktail parties and sporting occasions. We played for International Football matches at Wembley (including the FA Cup Final) and we were regulars at Twickenham for Rugby Internationals. Wimbledon, Henley, Lords and Ascot were all in the programme from time to time, as was the occasional booking to play at grounds such as Old Trafford (both cricket and football) and Anfield. It was a privileged life and, although you inevitably become a touch blasé when this is the daily norm, I did appreciate the opportunities that came my way.

Always in the background was the need to practice and improve as a musician. I was obsessive about music, especially classical music, and daily practice was essential for my peace of mind (still is). Even at this young age I had gained a huge amount of experience in all styles of music and, because of the nature of the work in Britannia, I had become particularly strong at Salon or Palm Court style music. Luckily there were always a few like-minded folk around me such as Rodney Preston, John Sharp, Dave Miles, Colin Brocklebank, John Hillier, Malcolm Kennard, Jack Kennedy and more.

Desperate to play some chamber music (which was not required in Britannia) four of us volunteered to play a string quartet at a lunchtime event in a hotel in (I think) Bermuda. We had chosen to play Antonín Dvořák's String Quartet in F major, Op. 96, nicknamed the 'American' Quartet. It was baking hot and we had to wait until the lunch had finished before we could start. It may have been a Rotary Lunch or something similar, I can't remember. By the time we started it was really hot and we were not in air conditioning. Within a few minutes the strings started to expand with the heat and sink in pitch so that intonation (tuning) became a struggle. Albeit we were fairly used to this happening, having been world travellers in hotter climes for some years, this was more of a problem in such a demanding (and long - almost 30 minutes) classical piece. The overwhelming sense of relief at getting to the end of the performance stays with me until this day. It must have sounded grim in places as you cannot entirely avoid using 'open' strings in this quartet, which exposed the tuning problems. Never again would I take on such a concert without knowing the conditions. We meant well!

John next to Lord and Lady Tavistock in Goldsmiths' Hall London
One of many Livery Company Dinners that we supported

CHAPTER 21

1972 - Another Momentous Year

Before the end of 1971 we all returned from leave early to prepare for another marathon tour, this time to Thailand, Malaysia, and Brunei via Madeira, Cape Town and Singapore. I had travelled to Portsmouth just after Christmas and stayed with John Hillier and his family in Copnor, Portsmouth for a couple of days prior to embarking in Britannia on 28th December. 1972 was also going to be notable for a reunion in Britannia with my old mate Alan Upton who joined the Yacht Band from HMS Eagle where he had been causing havoc for a couple of years. In the summer Alan and I joined forces with Lyn (Jamie) James to share a couple flats in Southsea - this did not end well! Jamie was blessed with outrageous good looks and a constant stream of girls appeared daily at our door looking for Jamie, either elated with excitement or distraught and about to commit suicide. This was the Jamie effect.

Later that summer I met Cay at a party, and within a few short months we were married on 16th December 1972. At that time Cay was serving in the WRNS and travelling the country as part of the Royal Marines Recruiting Display Team. Cay played the part of a defenceless girl, despatching Marines twice her size with her unarmed combat skills! She and I were based in the RM Barracks at Eastney.

But first we had a Royal Tour of some exciting places before us, including Malaysia, Thailand and Brunei all of which were firsts for me. Singapore was a vibrant place to say the least in the early 1970s. A few old hands in the band had served in one of the two Royal Marines bands permanently stationed in Singapore so knew the ropes of what and what not to do. Lee Kuan Yew was the first Prime Minister of Singapore, governing for three decades. Lee is recognised as the nation's founding father, with the country described as transitioning from a third world country to a first world country in a single generation under his leadership. This process was barely underway during our early visits and you could see every aspect of human behaviour before your very eyes when walking the streets.

The famous Bugis Street was renowned internationally from the 1950s to the 1980s for its nightly gathering of transvestites and transsexuals, a phenomenon that made it one of Singapore's[23] most notable destinations for foreign visitors during that period. Of course this was high on our list to see and it did not disappoint! Amongst the many highlights of our visit to Singapore was an opportunity for the band to play a short concert at the renowned Raffles Hotel

---

[23] On returning to Singapore in 1992 the original Bugis Street was now a cobblestoned, relatively wide avenue sandwiched between the buildings of the Bugis Junction shopping complex. It had lost its special charm.

which was great stuff. There is nothing quite like the sensation of sitting in a bar/restaurant in a warm and humid street, drinking a 'Tiger' beer and watching the world pass by. We did a lot of this.

Thailand

Needless to say the Royal programme went like clockwork after the Queen embarked in Sattahip, Thailand on 9th February. The usual format of cocktail party followed by the band Beating Retreat on the jetty under lights had the locals completely bewitched. This was always followed by a large number of engagements ashore when the band would perform at events to show the 'flag' and support the Royals. We had some spare time in Sattahip when the Royal Party left for events further inland. I remember a few of us hired horses and rode around the town like John Wayne and friends. We tied up the horses outside a bar and went in for a drink just like the movies - amazing. I also remember Sattahip for eating the hottest curry I have ever eaten, so much so that it burned the inside of my mouth and I couldn't play the trumpet for a week - good news for music lovers I hear you say!

The Royal Party of the Queen and Prince Philip also included Princess Anne and Lord Louis Mountbatten a great supporter of the Royal Marines Band. One of Lord Louis's sayings was that "The Royal Marines Band is my best weapon in peacetime". I often quoted him in later life when trying to justify keeping bands. Being around the last Viceroy of India was like being in a living history. On the few occasions I met up with old school friends when on leave, and they asked what I did, I sometimes explained a little of the above. I looked into their eyes and could see they didn't believe a word of what I was saying, so I gave up saying anything at all about life in Britannia. It was so far removed from the life they led I could understand their disbelief. For the same reasons I have rarely mentioned to others this part of my early life, even now.

Malaysia

The tour continued with visits to Singapore (again), Malacca, Port Klang (both in Malaysia), The Sembilan Islands, followed by Penang, The

Rear Admiral Trowbridge (Flag Officer Royal Yachts) welcoming Princess Anne
© *Crown copyright*

Maldives and Gan before sailing for the Seychelles and Mauritius in late March. Penang in Malaysia had the same feel as Singapore and retained its special character long after Singapore had undergone 'gentrification', as I discovered on another visit in the 1990s.

Each destination received the same programme of formal receptions, cocktail parties, Beating Retreats by the Band and a full programme of Royal visits ashore. In truth it was an exhausting schedule for The Queen and Prince Philip, yet they took it all in their stride whereas us mere mortals would have been dead on our feet. Royal Duty finished in Mauritius from where The Queen flew back to the UK. Britannia began her voyage home via Simonstown (South Africa), St Helena and Madeira before arriving back in Portsmouth on 30th April. One major bonus for us was the need to have essential maintenance carried out on the Britannia's boiler whilst in the Naval Dockyard at Simonstown, South Africa. This procedure took ten days or so during which time we were free to explore, and in the golfers case we took up almost permanent residence at Clovelly Golf Course, a beautiful course a few miles up the coast. As always we were made very welcome by the members who treated us like celebrities.

On the Sunday morning we were invited to play the small golf course at Simonstown. It was basically a large field with little or no trees or features. Anyway we started about 11am and were making our way around the course with our hosts when at 12 noon a loud bell rang out over the course and everyone started walking back to the clubhouse. This was explained away to us as a local custom so we dutifully followed our hosts. On arrival, the bar was in full session and we were plied with all manner of drinks which carried on for the next few hours. Apparently this was their Sunday ritual of playing a few token holes of golf as a ruse for a serious booze-up thereafter. Of course we entered into to the spirit of the occasion - as you do!

The Days of Hammocks and Camp Beds are over!

After a summer of smaller tours to the Channel Islands, Cowes week and the Western Isles Cruise the Yacht returned to Portsmouth on 11th August to start a major refit. At last we were to return the hammocks and camp beds that had been the norm since 1953!

The principal objective of the refit was to upgrade the quality of the accommodation for the Royal Yachtsmen, which had been the subject of criticism by a parliamentary delegation the previous year. The upgrading work included installing air conditioning, for which previously the port holes (scuttles) were opened, the installation of dining halls, previously Yachtsmen carried food to their Mess Decks, better recreation spaces and refurbished bathrooms. The biggest change was from sleeping in hammocks and camp beds to bunks. By 1972 Britannia had been the last ship in the RN in which sailors slept in hammocks.

The refit took almost one year to complete and it wasn't until July 1973 that it was possible to return to Britannia to make ready for the summer programme of Cowes and The Western Isles Tour in August. The band had left Britannia completely for the refit and moved back to Royal Marines Barracks Eastney to join the larger band. Towards the end of this period it was announced that Britannia was to be used by Princess Anne and Captain Mark Phillips for their Honeymoon to the West Indies in the autumn. This honeymoon trip was to be the start of another major 6-month global deployment.

The Royal Yacht Band rehearsal on The Veranda Deck - 1971
When Britannia was anchored off, unable to dock in remote islands we gave a marching display (Beating Retreat) in this small space after cocktail parties.

CHAPTER 22

Princess Anne and Captain Mark Phillips - Honeymoon Trip

During the Autumn months Britannia would be used for the honeymoon of Princess Anne and Captain Mark Phillips, followed by Royal duty in support of the Commonwealth Games in New Zealand, and then a tour of Australia, Indonesia and Pacific Islands. To add a further complication for us, the band would sail from Portsmouth in Britannia, spend the Honeymoon period in the West Indies with the Royal couple, fly back to the UK for a busy Christmas schedule, then fly out to New Zealand at the end of December to join Britannia in Auckland prior to the Commonwealth Games in January and the onward tour. Piece of cake!

The Royal Wedding was on 14th November while Britannia was preparing itself in Barbados for the arrival of the married couple the next day. There was huge interest in the wedding in the West Indies. Although the islands were relatively inaccessible and chosen for privacy, they were teeming with reporters. The idea was to cruise around the islands and find a few remote beaches for some time ashore. Unfortunately the Yacht was observed and the secret was blown, so it turned into a game of cat and mouse over the next two weeks. After cruising the Caribbean the Yacht entered the Panama Canal and then onwards to the Galapagos Islands for a third visit since 1970. Further stops at Pitcairn Island and Fiji completed the first part of this marathon tour. The Band had flown back to the UK at the end of November to take part in a busy domestic programme of events leading up to Christmas.

Princess Anne and Captain Mark Phillips during their Honeymoon
© Crown copyright

Commonwealth Games (Christchurch NZ, 1974)

Up Spirits!

Our next challenge was to get to Auckland New Zealand by the start of January to rejoin the Yacht for the Commonwealth Games stage of the tour. Today this might be a routine matter, but 45 years ago this proved a convoluted process taking a little over three days to arrive in Auckland at 2359hrs on New Year's Eve!! By this time we were fairly cheesed off and just wanted to find a bed and start again the next day. Unfortunately, being New Year's Eve, and landing on the stroke of midnight, our best laid plans fell apart and there was no Naval Liaison reception or transport to take us to the Naval Base in Auckland, Devonport Naval Base - HMNZS Philomel. To cut the story short we eventually arrived at Philomel around 4am to a bewildered skeleton duty crew who were not expecting us. After a few short-tempered exchanges we were found some bedding and beds and all tipped in for a few hours - heaven.

The Yacht was not due to arrive in Auckland until 3rd January so we woke the next day to a damage limitation exercise of finding some decent accommodation for the next two nights and organising our equipment. Needless to say, morale was not high. However, around mid-morning we were gathered together to confirm our personal details, including DOBs, for our hosts. Someone asked why this was necessary as all this information must have been forwarded long before we arrived, to which the answer was, 'We need to know as you are all victualled in for 'Tot' at lunchtime'. What we had no idea of was, although 'Tot' in the British Navy had ceased on 31st July 1970, it was to be 28th February 1990 when the final day of the rum ration in the Royal New Zealand Navy took place. Hooray!

In all my years in the RMs I have never witnessed such a complete reversal of morale as was the case with this simple piece of information. By 1pm we were all sitting around enjoying some Navy Rum and planning the next two days run ashore in Auckland. That's life in a 'blue suit'[24] right there!

The time in Auckland turned out well for the band as there were problems with the paintwork of the hull of Britannia that had to be corrected before she could sail for Christchurch and the Commonwealth Games. This meant a free week in Auckland, which was a rare opportunity enjoyed by all.

---

[24] A term commonly used by Royal Marines to justify the wide and unexpected variety of circumstances that occur in the course of normal duty.

CHAPTER 23

Christchurch

After the 1970 trip to New Zealand I had visited my sister Margie and her husband Mick singing the praises of life in New Zealand, and enthusiastic about emigrating there one day. Low and behold, within two years Margie and Mick had emigrated to NZ and were living in Christchurch! So their house became our base for the next few weeks with regular visits when we were not working. In fact we undertook very few engagements once the Games had started as it was generally the custom for the host nation to provide all the entertainment and music ashore during Royal visits. So it was golf and sightseeing with the odd party thrown into the mix. I think it was during this time that The New Zealand Broadcasting Orchestra gave a gala concert for the Queen's Visit and we managed to get some tickets. The soprano soloist was a young Maori student named Kiri Te Kanawa who rather stole the show. She would go on to do this many times on the world stage - what a talent!

Heading North

The Queen closed the games on 2nd February and so began the rest of their Tour of New Zealand calling at Whangarei, Waitangi and Auckland (again) before sailing north for the Tour of the Pacific Islands. Norfolk Island was followed by Pentacost Island where the Queen was invited to witness the traditional 'bungee' type jump where young men attach a vine to their ankles and dive head-first from an 80-foot tower. This traditional ritual required huge courage and tempted daredevils to dive ever closer to the ground. On this most important day tragedy struck and one of the young men dived from the tower with vines that were too long, hitting the ground and receiving fatal head injuries. Apparently such accidents are rare given the risks and this tragedy rather soured the visit.

Later that day the Yacht sailed for Santo and The Solomon Islands. As with all sea crossings the Royals and the Ship's company invented novel ways to entertain themselves and a memorable concert on the foc'sle was arranged entitled 'Round the World

The local custom on Pentacost Island to prove manhood. Sometimes with fatal consequences.

Members of Ship's Company concert party
Dressed as Maori Warriors

in Eighty Ways'. The band always provided the accompaniment and 'fillers' to pad out the concert with others doing their 'party-piece'. I shall always remember Lord Mountbatten leading the 'Haka' dressed as a Maori warrior. As with everything he did, Lord Louis threw himself into the role with gusto, including all the correct words - apparently. What a night to be part of though.

During the Tour of the Solomon Islands we visited Guadalcanal, Gizo and Bourgainville Islands before heading for Darwin to be ready to receive other members of the Royal Party who had been carrying out a different programme of events around Australia using aircraft. I liked Darwin as it had the feel of a frontier town about it, with lots of wooden buildings and so remote from the rest of Australia that it felt almost like a separate country. We were welcomed with open arms and the band played in a couple of bars in the evenings for the princely sum of free beer! Later that year Cyclone Tracy, a tropical cyclone, devastated the town from 24th–26th December 1974 after which Darwin was rebuilt to modern standards. For visitors, it was a shame in some ways to change such a unique place.

Indonesia

After a few days at sea we arrived in Bali to await the arrival of The Queen, who had flown back to the UK a couple of weeks before as The Prime Minister Edward Heath had called a snap General Election. Once safely back, and after a day of Royal engagements in Bali, the Yacht sailed for Tanjong Priok, the Port for Jakarta. The unforgettable drive from Tanjong Priok into Jakarta followed the shore of the main river running through the city. The band was the first group ashore to play for an engagement in the city and were mesmerised by the complete range of human activities that took place in and alongside that river for its complete length. Washing clothes, bathing, ablutions of all types (including toilet activities), fishing - you name it. It wasn't possible to drive more than a few minutes without witnessing a bare bottom or two. As there was no other route into town the Royal Party must also have enjoyed these greetings - so funny!

Scary Stuff!

Two further memorable Jakarta events remain with me to this day. The first was three large packing cases of anklungs[25] arriving on the jetty for the Director of Music. The Queen had witnessed a concert played on anklungs at the Presidential Palace during their stay in Jakarta and Prince Philip had managed to persuade their owners that the RM Band in Britannia would dearly love to have a set for them to play onboard. Presumably meant in a jokey way, they nevertheless turned up. Jim Mason invited The Queen to inspect the anklungs on the jetty and apparently she said, "They look very nice. Please can you play them at tonight's dinner in the Embassy?" A couple of hours of relative panic ensued during which we were allocated our various notes in order to play the hymn 'Abide with me'. I had the note 'A' which happens to be the first note in the hymn. To make the note sound you need to shake the ankklung vigorously for the duration you need the note to sound. We assembled in the Junior Rates recreation space for the rehearsal and set off with 'Abide with Me'. In truth it was very simple to put this together, so by the second run through we had cracked it. For luck, we had one final run through, so I set off with my 'A' first note, when, to my absolute horror, the most menacing looking spider fell from one of the bamboo tubes and landing on my knee (we were in shorts) and started to do press-ups whilst glaring at me!

Although we were in a confined space, I lost the plot and panicked, dropping the anklung, knocked over the music stand and bolted for the door. The spider must have been as frightened as me and leapt off my knee and made for the secluded corner of the recreation space. The rest of the band, not realising or seeing what had occurred, responded to my panic by panicking themselves, knocking over everything in their way and trying to follow me towards the exit. Chaos reigned for what seemed a long time. Eventually a nervous calm returned and we started looking for the spider which we, by now, had decided was the deadliest creature known to man! You may have detected that I do not like spiders a great deal. The moral of this story is 'always be nervous if someone asks you to shake a piece of unfumigated bamboo over your lap in the tropics'. We survived - just. The spider ain't no more!

The second memory is also insect related. Jakarta is home to many and varied crawling and flying creatures one of which is a giant-size moth that was attracted to the lights on Britannia's upper deck. While in harbour Britannia is floodlit to make a striking spectacle from the shore and for these moths the lights were irresistible. One evening I was watching a movie in the Recreation space and fully engrossed in the film when some wag, having captured one of these giant moths, opened the door slightly and released the creature into the darkness of this makeshift cinema. The recreation space was tiny and it was crammed with 30 plus movie

---

[25] The *angklung* is a musical instrument from Indonesia made of a varying number of bamboo tubes attached to a bamboo frame. The tubes are carved to have a resonant pitch when struck and are tuned to octaves, similar to Western handbells.

85

watchers when the giant moth took to the air and found itself in the projection lights to the screen, which magnified its already menacing size several times. To make things worse its wings made a loud noise. Once again, chaos reigned and everyone was climbing over each other for the door having no idea what this huge flying monster in the room was. The room was dark for the movie so there was genuine panic - I can personally vouch for this! In due course, lights were turned on, the movie turned off, and the room cleared while one of the braver souls captured the moth and released it through one of the port holes. Alfred Hitchcock would have been proud of creating such tension in a film!

Royal Duty for this trip finished in Malaysia and after the Royals had left to fly back to the UK we started the long trip home via stops in Singapore, Mauritius, St Helena, Dakar and Casablanca, reaching Portsmouth on 3rd May. Cowes week and The Western Isles Cruise to Balmoral completed Royal Duties this year, after which I was drafted to Deal to undertake the 8-week BdSgts Music Course (The M1 Course). The course at this time was under the guidance of the composer Michael Hurd for all the academic work, which was an unexpected bonus. My first taste of classroom work since leaving school ten years earlier!

Ever keen to join in, Lord Louis on a visit to the
RMSM Deal in the mid 1970s

CHAPTER 24

My Final Royal Tour in Britannia

My final tour in Britannia was to the Caribbean, Central America and the USA, leaving Portsmouth in late January 1975 and heading for Mexico via Madeira, Antigua and Nassau where we had four days to explore before the Royal Party arrived. Our port of call in Mexico was Vera Cruz having landed the Queen at Cozumel en route to commence the Royal Tour by air. The programme of events in Mexico was complex and required part of the Band (a small orchestra) to fly the 200 miles to Mexico City to play for formal engagements in the British Embassy over a 3-day period. The Mexican President was keen to impress for the Royal visit so he sent his personal executive jet to take the sixteen of us on this short hop flight into Mexico City, complete with all the VIP treatment reserved for more lofty guests.

On arrival in Mexico City we were taken to our hotel accommodation then immediately onward to the British Embassy where we rehearsed for the formal dinner to take place that evening. What none of us had realised was that Mexico City is 7,200 feet above sea level, which is a serious altitude from the sea level at Vera Cruz, and it takes some getting used to. The lack of oxygen at this height really started to kick in as we began our programme of music for the arrival of VIPs for the reception prior to the dinner. Typical symptoms of altitude sickness can be tiredness, dizziness, headaches, sickness or worse. Apparently our playing was very dodgy to the point where guests were asking is the orchestra OK, they sound as if they're drunk! Things didn't get much better as we stumbled our way through the evening's dinner music. Our Director Jim Mason recalls the evening as one of the most bizarre of his long and varied career, especially as we were stone cold sober!

On returning to Vera Cruz another round of formal events, including a State Banquet in Britannia for the President of Mexico, completed this whistle-stop tour of the country. Our next destinations were the Central American countries of Belize, Honduras and Costa Rico where the familiar routines of Cocktail Parties, Dinners and events ashore happened almost by automation. The next formal Royal event was to be the Commonwealth Heads of Government Meeting in Jamaica towards the end of April, which left a little over three weeks to fill. Certainly not time enough to return to the UK, so an impromptu visit to New Orleans to 'show the flag' was arranged followed by a 10-day routine maintenance visit to Bermuda. Sweet!

These little bonus visits with little or no work made the whole experience of being a 'Yachtie' so special. New Orleans was an iconic city with so much history, especially with the British who were not always welcome. Bermuda was just idyllic, with beautiful weather, golf courses and stunning scenery along the South of the Island. We hired 50cc motorbikes most days to explore the islands and when not doing this we played golf along the mix of courses that pepper the South Coast. Terrific. It was almost resented when we had to sail for Jamaica to resume Royal Duties as The Queen arrived back in Britannia on 26th April. The Commonwealth Heads of Government Meeting was always a priority for the Queen who saw the Commonwealth as one of the great pillars of stability in the world. Her knack of bringing world leaders together to talk and get to know each other was inspired and solved many potential problems before they became bigger issues. Her unique style and long years of experience, coupled with her reputation for confidentiality made her a unique sounding board for world leaders to discuss their concerns. I was lucky enough to be on the periphery for a number of these occasions.

The Commonwealth Heads of Government Meeting in Britannia. Harold Wilson PM
© Crown copyright

Apart from a few smaller 'one-off' events in Britannia that summer my time in The Yacht was at an end, although I didn't realise it at the time. I was nominated to undertake the 1-year Bandmasters' Course held at the Royal Marines School of Music starting in early 1976. This was the long hot summer when it didn't rain from February until October in the South East, other than 18th June when my sister-in-law Rebecca married Dave and it rained all day! I always believed that I would return to Portsmouth and Royal Yacht service, but it never happened. Even in later years when I was appointed as Director of Music of the 'Royal' Band in 1998, the Yacht had been decommissioned the previous year and put out to rest in Leith Scotland as a tourist attraction. For me, it just wasn't to be.

CHAPTER 25

The Bandmasters' Course

The Bandmasters' Course lasts for one year and takes place in the Higher Training Department of the Royal Marines School of music. There are normally between three to six RM students plus the occasional Foreign & Commonwealth student. The main training is as a conductor, with composition and arranging, harmony and counterpoint, aural training and history of music making up the remainder of the syllabus. This content has remained broadly the same since the formation of the RM Band Service in the early 1950s, although the syllabus has been kept up-to-date by the Academic Professor of Music down the years. Today (and for the past 25 years) the Academic Professor is Dr Liz Le Grove, a highly talented organist who is a square peg in a square hole. Liz has done wonders for the department over many years and she is central to the success of the modern Band Service.

For my Bandmasters' Course in 1976 the Academic Professor was Alan Ramel, a former school teacher. Alan was probably a very good school teacher, but he had no background or expertise in conducting or composition/orchestration, the main elements of this course, so these subjects were left to others. In truth, Alan was not a good fit for this post and I believe he found the military humour a bit close to the bone for his taste. However, I liked Alan personally and learned all I could about harmony and counterpoint from him, plus the history of Western Music, which was his strong area. The 2 x SNCO Instructors in Higher Training were WO2 Bandmaster Earnest Ward (RIP) who mostly looked after the administration of the department, and Band Colour Sergeant Phil Hughes[26] (RIP) a talented pianist, conductor and all-round

1976/77 Bandmasters' Class

[26] Phil went on to become a superb Corps Bandmaster.

musician. Between them they filled the gaps in the teaching to make for a good learning experience. Phil's special strength was as a jazz/big band/cocktail pianist. He had a good 'ear' for music and was noted as an inventive arranger for band. I remained good friends with Phil down the years as we both still lived in Deal, and we got together for the occasional gig before Phil sadly passed away in 2019.

Other students on the course were, Peter Rutterford, Phil Fryer, Steve Cook, Stu Waite, plus an Australian Navy Chief Petty Officer named Vic Knowles who had to pass this course in order to become a commissioned officer back in Australia. Vic did pass the course and eventually went on to become the Principal Director of Music of the Royal Australian Navy. We have always kept in touch and have met in both England and Australia for holidays and the occasional beer!

The content of the Bandmasters' Course was, and is, superb, not least because there is a professional band/orchestra in place to practice your arrangements and conducting skills with. What other institution can boast this? A few years later while on the 1-year Conductor's Course at the Royal Academy of Music I recall just one conducting opportunity each week of about 30 minutes over only 36 weeks. Even then some of this time was poached by others or interrupted by half-terms and exams. At The RMSM the working year was 45 weeks long and the band/ orchestra was available (during the 1970s) several days each week through the Winter. There was also a series of eight public concerts at The School when the Bandmaster students would be fully involved with conducting. It allowed opportunities to try out your compositions and arrangements with professional players, which again was quite a privilege compared with other institutions. As mentioned earlier, I always had a good aural sense which helped with harmony, so these were exciting times for me as I had quickly realised that conducting was another strong area that I couldn't get enough of.

The upshot was that I came top of the Course (winning the Medal from The Worshipful Company of Musicians) and won the Boosey & Hawkes Cup and The Chappel Conducting Prize. I also passed the LGSM (violin teacher), the ARCM (conducting) and LRAM (conducting with a 95% pass mark, one of the highest ever awarded).

After the course I was expecting to return to Portsmouth and resume my previous role in Britannia, as I had been led to believe. However, it was with a bit of a disappointment that I was drafted to the Staff Band at Deal to lead the orchestra as the previous Leader (WO2 Bandmaster George Simpson) was due to retire. George and myself shared many mutual interests, most importantly Chamber Music in which we were to collaborate for many years in later life. George and I have been great friends down the years and we still occasionally bump into each other in Deal.

Anyway it was to be The Staff Band at Deal, which was not all bad as Cay and I had bought a small bungalow in the town a year earlier to get on the housing ladder. Cay was also pregnant with Nicholas who would be born on 25th August 1977. A great day. The only 'cock-up' was I took a bunch of Antirrhinums from our garden to the hospital, which turned out to be housing the 'mother nest' of a colony of earwigs. Matron was not best pleased, so she red-carded me!

We kept the bungalow for six years and extended it twice to become a 4-bedroom home with a large private garden in which we built a 90-yard golf hole - much to the horror of our neighbours! Our son Stephen was born on 8th July 1978, so we were a perfect fit for the house.

Staff Band Cricket Team 1978 - Bob Simmonds (RIP) (Team Captain with shield)
I always kept wicket

CHAPTER 26

Staff Band - Back to the violin

One good thing about joining the Staff Band in May 1977 was that I knew all the members of the band as I had just finished a year conducting them regularly as a member of the Bandmasters' Course. Also a large number of them were direct contemporaries of mine from training.

Our first notable assignment was to be sent to Glasgow on 'Green Goddess' fire trucks to cover the first fireman's strike in the Autumn of 1978. Glasgow had the worst fire record in Europe at the time, so to send in the Deal and Plymouth Bands with obsolete Green Goddess fire trucks to save the day was a little bizarre. It was November when we were deployed to Glasgow where our accommodation was a primary school in Pollock with limited washing facilities and toilets sized for primary age children. This was to be our home for the next two months as it turned out.

We named our fire truck 'Trumpton' and we reported each day with our adopted names of Pugh, Pugh, Barney, McGrew, Cuthbert, Dibble, Grubb. We had received one afternoon's training in fighting fires at Chatham Fire School where they had proper firefighting equipment, none of which we had on the Green Goddesses, so the message was once again 'adapt and overcome'. We had many a laugh on our 'shouts' and I am sure we made things worse and not better in some cases, but we did try hard to do the right thing and it was pure luck we didn't have any major fires to deal with. Fires in skips, chip pan fires and false alarms were the most common. Our most successful rescue was of an elderly couple who were on the first floor of their house watching their favourite television programme while their house burned around them. Had we not dragged them out I am sure they would have sat there and burned!

Anyway, it was good news for me to be returned to Deal just before Christmas, not least because Cay was at home with two young babies with whooping cough.

Back to Deal

During the Autumn and Winter terms the Staff Band programme was centred around eight orchestral concerts given in the main Concert Hall or the barracks church. For me these were the highlights and an opportunity to play the orchestral repertoire

En route to Glasgow for firefighting.
L to R: John Perkins, Pete Rose, Martin Dale, Ray Mosley, Trevor Attwood

92

that I favoured. The repertoire under Paul Neville was always challenging with symphonies, concertos, and any number of miscellaneous orchestral works. There was also one concert each year given over to a major Choral work, such as The Dream of Gerontius, The Messiah, Handel's Coronation Anthems and various requiems. This was the only place in The Band Service where an orchestral season took place and it didn't suit everyone. However, for the majority of us, we loved it.

Subsequent PDMs continued this orchestral tradition, which provided the likes of me opportunities to perform a number of violin concertos including those by Mendelssohn, Bruch, Mozart, Bach and others. The most challenging concert I can recall during this period was when Lt Col Jim Mason invited his two predecessors, Lt Col Sir Vivian Dunn and Lt Col Paul Neville, to share the conducting with him in a marathon concert. At this time I was the WO2 Bandmaster of the Staff Band and Leader of the Orchestra, so I also had to coordinate the rehearsal schedule with the conductors who could not have been more different characters. I had served with them both so knew them well. Sir Vivian had chosen William Walton's Coronation March 'Orb and Sceptre' and a suite of music which he had penned himself on an Arabic theme. Both these pieces were challenging enough. However, Paul Neville had chosen just one piece, 'Scheherazade' - the whole of it! Scheherazade could in many ways be described as a concerto for orchestra, as all sections of the orchestra have demanding parts. However, it is without doubt a violin concerto and one of the most demanding solo violin parts in the repertoire. Jim Mason finished the concert off with a Tchaikovsky waltz which felt like light relief. What a concert!

Lt Col Hoskins (right), PDM designate, with his three predecessors
prior to the Scheherazade concert

The other central part of the programme was recordings which mainly took place at Abbey Road Studios London on the EMI label. Engineer Stuart Eltham and Producer Bob Barrett were the production team and my appetite for the recording process was insatiable. There is no doubt that the forensic rehearsals to prepare for a recording do wonders for the standard of playing in the band and I always made sure we made at least one new recording each year when I became a Director of Music. Similarly, as many radio broadcasts as possible.

The summer terms were mostly given over to the large-scale outdoor marching events such as The Royal Tournament, Edinburgh Tattoo, Massed Bands Beating Retreat on Horseguards Parade or other London ceremonial. Every second year we travelled to Toronto Canada for the Canadian National Exhibition, which was a fun trip in the scorching summer temperatures Canada enjoys. Around 600 bagpipers made this an experience unlike any other!

A year in London

In the summer of 1980, and somewhat out of the blue, I was nominated to attend the 1-year conductor's course at the Royal Academy of Music London. At the time this course was the professional musical training for potential Directors of Music, although not all who undertook this course went on to become DOMs. It was a terrific opportunity to study in the country's premier music conservatoire, and importantly in a completely orchestral setting. My joint first studies were conducting and composition. The conducting professor was Maurice Miles, an aloof man who was quite elderly and fell asleep often when we were conducting! Maurice had been a guest conductor at Deal a number of times, so we knew each other. My composition teacher was Malcolm McDonald, a superb all-round musician whose special interest was jazz piano. Malcolm was a practical musician who had worked as the Deputy Conductor of the Cape Town Symphony Orchestra and a wide range of other jobs where he was required to compose and arrange to order. I looked forward to the time I had with Malcolm and I considered him a friend, who I kept in contact with until he passed away a decade later. The more contemporary composition teacher at the time was Paul Patterson who was into electronic and 'squeaky door' experimental music. Paul changed direction musically sometime later and has produced some superb compositions over the years, but, at that time his lectures did not interest me. After a few weeks I gave up going to his presentations believing that life was too short for contemporary music!

The conducting syllabus at the Academy was well structured, starting with the baroque period and rapidly working through the Classical and Romantic repertoire, even choral works. We never touched upon 20th Century Music. I learned a lot from Maurice and his short book on conducting 'Are you Beating Two or Four' is a very useful start point for any budding conductor. The highlight of my time on this course was conducting Brahms' 4th Symphony. I also managed to get the violin recognised as a second study for me and I was allocated Jack McDougal as my violin teacher. Again I got on really well with Jack and studied the Brahms Violin Concerto and Saint-Saëns Introduction & Rondo Capriccioso, both of which I gave performances with piano accompaniment. I think my violin playing in these years was as good as it got and I felt as if I could sight read and play most everything put in front of me. A nice feeling.

After the Academy course finished in June 1981 I was drafted to the Band of The Britannia Royal Naval College Dartmouth as the second-in-command in the rank of Band Colour Sergeant. This cameo appearance saw me playing for Newton Abbot carnival and some background music for one of the Wardroom dinners, after which we were all sent on six weeks annual summer leave which was the Dartmouth schedule. While back in Deal on leave I received news that I had been promoted Warrant Officer 2 Bandmaster and drafted back to the Staff Band as the Bandmaster! I remember driving back to Dartmouth to collect my belongings listening to the Ashes Headingley Test Match where Ian Botham was on fire. I got so engrossed in the match and Botham's innings that I had to pull over into a lay-by and sit and listen, as to continue driving was dangerous! 1981 Botham's Ashes, what a fantastic series of matches - buy the DVD.

Lt Col Paul Neville's final performance on 'Pebble Mill at One' in 1978.
(BdSgt) John back far right on trumpet

CHAPTER 27

Bandmaster, Staff Band

On return to Deal I rejoined the Staff Band as the WO2 Bandmaster with my old boss from Royal Yacht days Lt Col Jim Mason as The PDM. The band was busy as Jim's bands always were. Jim believed that we should be out on the road performing concerts and other quality gigs, quite often on the London Hotel scene or national sporting events etc. Mostly these were fee-paying events so zero cost to the tax payer, but more importantly it gave us a high profile in the community. It was a happy band under Jim's leadership and we still managed to keep the orchestral series of concerts going throughout the Autumn and Winter terms. Jim was clever when it came to getting others to do the musical things he was not so strong at himself. He enjoyed seeing others doing well and playing to their strengths, all part of the development process which ultimately he was responsible for. Not all his successors possessed this vision as I was to find to my cost, but for the moment, life was sweet.

In the November I undertook The Director of Music exams, which was the professional qualification for Captain (today's Major equivalent) and Director of Music of a Staff band. The written papers were set and marked by the Royal Academy of Music and the conducting and viva voce took place in Deal with the Staff Band and visiting adjudicators. My orchestral conducting piece was a public performance of Brahms' 4th Symphony and my concert band piece, which took place the following morning, was the band transcription of Rimsky Korsakov's Scheherazade. I achieved an overall pass mark of 82% which qualified me professionally all the way to Principal Director of Music.

Life as Bandmaster of the Staff Band was busy yet varied and challenging. Apart from the music (violin and conducting), which was my strong area, there was a considerable amount of administration involved with the job as the band numbered over 60 members. We were constantly up and down to London for events both big and small, ranging from London Ceremonial duties in Buckingham Palace to many dinners and entertainments in City Livery Companies and West End hotels. I got along well with Jim Mason so it was sad for us when his time to leave came

The Staff Band SNCOs dining out
Jim and Alice Mason - 1982

around in early 1982, after four years[27] as PDM. His successor was Lt Col Graham Hoskins another old colleague from Royal Yacht days.

Graham took a fresh look at the structure of the setup in Deal and decided that The Corps Bandmaster (Phil Hughes) should give up his position as Chief Instructor in Higher Training to join The Headquarters. Phil would be replaced by me, thus removing me as Bandmaster of the Staff Band, which may have been Graham's real aim! However, Graham did invite me back to play the Mendelssohn Violin Concerto at a concert with him conducting which I enjoyed greatly and our relationship was good - still is. Indeed he was instrumental in me being promoted to both WO1 and Commissioned as he was on the Promotion Board for both. Thanks.

Chief Instructor, Higher Training

Although primarily known as a performer, especially as a violinist, I was also strong as a conductor and an improving composer/arranger, so the prospect of taking over from my good friend Phil Hughes as the Chief Instructor in Higher Training appealed to me. I enjoyed classroom teaching and felt I could add something useful to get student bandmasters thinking about how best to be effective as a conductor. My emphasis was always to teach the basics thoroughly and keep conducting simple and clear. Every now and then someone comes along who has a real talent for conducting, they will find their way, but most are 'grafters' so a functional technique is the best answer.

My number two in the department was Band Colour Sergeant Joe Baggs, a gentle giant of a man who loved his music and would happily talk all day about the finer details of any given piece. We had great fun teaching the courses that came through the department and the sense of humour of staff and students kept the mood light and constructive.

The most important subject was conducting which took place with the Staff Band as part of the eight Winter orchestral public concerts. Each course always had at least two or more Foreign and Commonwealth students who had been sent to us from countries such as Nigeria, Iran, Pakistan, Australasia, Sri Lanka and Malaysia for example. Quite often these overseas students had no background of Western Art Music and in many cases had never seen an orchestra in the flesh before! Some could barely speak English before arriving. Most all of them had a mountain to climb, so it was a question of teaching them as best we could, taking into account their strengths and weaknesses.

I remember clearly a student from Nigeria who came as part of the Bandmasters' Course. He had no prior experience in conducting or western music and was completely ill-suited to this

---

[27] The optimum length of time for a PDM in my view. No more than five years to keep things fresh.

course. However we had to do what we could as the MOD received considerable funds from training overseas students. I had toiled long and hard with this student to help him prepare for his first public performance with the orchestra, which was to be the overture, 'The Calif of Bagdad'. It goes without saying that the most important aspects of conducting are starting and stopping a piece. This particular overture starts slowly and quietly with an anacrusis[28] of one quaver. I had drilled into him to count in his mind the speed of the quaver beat and when he was satisfied that all was quiet give a preparatory beat after which the orchestra would begin playing. We had practiced this many times in the classroom and a number of times with the orchestra. What could possibly go wrong?

I was looking through the window in the concert hall door after sending him on stage to conduct. He received polite applause as he approached the rostrum where he bowed to the audience then turned around to face the orchestra. So far so good. Before anything else could happen, the Leader (I think John Pring) of the orchestra asked the oboist to play an 'A' for the orchestra to retune prior to starting 'The Calif of Bagdad'. This completely threw our newbie conductor out of his stride as he believed the orchestra had started without him - argh! He took an almighty swing with his (fibreglass!) baton, that I could hear going through the air outside of the concert hall, and he was off with his baton solo. The orchestra was dumfounded, fell into silence, and we all watched with shock horror as he continued the performance by himself without any music! OMG! After a very awkward 30 seconds or so, the leader of the orchestra stopped him and had him start again. I was clawing at the outside of the door cursing my luck for not factoring in the tune-up. I still wake at nights, almost 40 years on, reliving that moment!

Warrant Officer First Class - Just

In 1983, while serving as The Chief Instructor in Higher Training, another unexpected turn of events was about to change my whole career, although it started quite by chance.

At this time there was just one Warrant Officer Bandmaster (1st Class) whose job title was 'The Corps Bandmaster'. The incumbent was WO1 Phil Hughes, a close friend 10 years my senior. Phil was retiring aged 42 years. The promotion to Corps Bandmaster was the reserve of a senior Bandmaster coming towards the end of their career as it was a last job before retiring, there being nowhere else to go beyond that job. I had thought nothing about this because I was far too young. However, the selection process was held at the RM Headquarters at Eastney Portsmouth together with potential RSMs and other WO1s in the wider Corps. The process included two written papers discussing general knowledge and military/Corps related questions. You also had to write an essay. This was followed on the final day by an interview before a board of senior

---

[28] The anacrusis is an introductory measure - a note or series of notes coming before the first complete measure of a composition.

officers. At the end of the final day you were asked back in before the board to be told whether you had passed or not. All very black and white; no discussion, in or out!

Three senior Bandmasters were nominated to attend the board, all friends of mine, albeit five or more years older than me, and this whole process was underway without me really noticing as it didn't affect me.

A couple of days before the board was due to convene I was sent for by The PDM who said that he needed another WO2 to attend the board as one of the candidates had dropped out, and I was the only person available as others, more suited age-wise, were either abroad or involved with essential duties. The PDM made it clear that I was being sent to make up the numbers and to gain some experience for a future board. Fair enough. I knew both remaining candidates for this board as both had served with me in The Royal Yacht years earlier and were good mates. We all assumed that WO2 Mick Howarth (RIP) would get this promotion as he was about 38 years old (ideal), very experienced and a popular character in the Band Service. I called Mick and explained the situation that I was along for the ride, and he invited me to come and stay with him and Carrie in Portsmouth for the three days of the board. This I gladly accepted as time spent with Mick usually meant a few beers and lively chat, and we had plenty to reminisce about. You can see where this is going - The Board came and went and at the end I went before the President to be told that I had passed the Board and would be promoted later that year to replace Phil Hughes as The Corps Bandmaster.

This was not meant to happen! Further, it was a job that I didn't want as it was mostly administration and I wanted to stay in music where I was already enjoying what I was doing. I also believed Mick would have made an ideal Corps Bandmaster, better than me at that time, as it played to his strengths. I couldn't really enjoy the moment as much as I should have because I felt slightly guilty at having been selected in place of Mick with whom I was staying! It was a little awkward to say the least, but Mick was gracious as ever.

As the months unfolded towards my promotion to WO1 later in 1983 it transpired that I was the youngest (at 32 years) WO1 to be selected since the Second World War and I was destined to be in this job for ten years. Shock horror!

The thought of me blocking this post for such a long time obviously started to occur to others and I was brought forward to attend a Special Duties (SD) Selection Board for promotion to Commissioned Officer. This I did in the Autumn of 1983 and was duly selected to undertake the 3-month SD Course at the Commando Training Centre Lympstone Devon, starting in January 1984. So, quite by chance, I became the first WO1 Bandmaster to be commissioned, a record that stands to this day - well they had to do something with me!

CHAPTER 28

Special Duties Officer (SD) Course

It was by no means certain that attending the SD Course at the Commando Training Centre at Lympstone meant automatic promotion, and, although six of us started, only five passed and were commissioned[29].

Unusually there were two WO1s, me and RSM Dave Chisnell, former RSM of 42 Commando during the Falklands conflict. This was the first time WO1s had undertaken the course, and considered as letting the side down by some SNCOs at the time. Others included WO2 Terry Sparkes (whose father was Bill Sparkes, one of the original Cockleshell Heroes), a Platoon Weapons Instructor (PWI) and great character, WO2 Mike Snow, Intelligence Corps expert and impressive all-round guy, Sgt Dick Brocklehurst helicopter pilot who was Brigadier Julian Thompson's pilot during the Falklands conflict. Finally there was a CSgt Drill Instructor who failed to complete the course.

The course (in those days) was a mix of military exercises such as 'night NAVEX' across Dartmoor, assault course, and similar trials and tribulations. In truth these elements represented

Special Duties Officer Course January 1984

---

[29] I believe the system is different now as candidates are promoted prior to the training. Seems the wrong way round to me!

a bit of an insult to the other five who were some of the most expert soldiers in the Armed Forces. However, for me, they were a challenge and I needed help from time to time. For instance, I was given command of the first leg of the night NAVEX across Dartmoor (in January in the rain!) and began by heading off in the wrong direction, thus making what was already a 20K plus exercise even further. I was quickly rescued by the others, which was just as well - for me, and them!

I remember one cold and wet overnight exercise on Woodbury Common (a training area close to Lympstone similar to Dartmoor) when in the middle of the night I was having a drink of tea talking to Terry Sparkes at the back of a Land Rover. Terry was alive with energy, eyes bright and morale high, clearly loving the environment we were in right then. For me it was bordering on dreadful, so I asked Terry how he remains so upbeat when only being bitten by a snake could have made things worse! He said, "Look around you John, this is my Albert Hall". Enough said, and thank God for people like Terry. Some weeks later I arranged a coach trip to the Royal Albert Hall for all the course members and the Instructional Staff to witness the famous Band Service 'Mountbatten Festival of Music'. Once settled in our box and enjoying a glass of wine prior to the concert starting, I stood up and said, causing much laughter, "Gentlemen, this is my Woodbury Common". Touché.

Other parts of the course were administrative which was plain sailing for me, being more used to classroom-based work than the others. The five of us who passed the course were a tight knit group and I enjoyed their company and friendship. Although all quite different characters they shared a common professional approach to everything they did and I was glad that the likes of them were 'on my side'.

On 2 March 1984 I was promoted 2nd Lieutenant, the first WO1 Bandmaster to be commissioned, and appointed as The Director of Music to Flag Officer Plymouth.

The Flag Officer Plymouth's Band
1985 in Liverpool

CHAPTER 29

First Command - Director of Music to Flag Officer Plymouth

They say that your first command is really special and you will never forget it. So true, but it did not start well for me; in fact it was a touch disastrous!

I joined HMS Raleigh as The Director of Music to Flag Officer Plymouth on a Tuesday in early May 1984. Having never served in a Royal Naval shore establishment before it was an exciting new adventure, my first command and miles from the Headquarters (just as I liked it!). Standing in the bar prior to dinner of the first night I got chatting to another new joiner, a tall young dentist by the name of Colin Priestland. As we talked I explained that I was taking over as the Director of Music which immediately sparked Colin's attention. He went on to explain that his father-in-law was a certain Lt Col Jim Mason, former Principal Director of Music and my old boss of many years! What a small world. Colin, wife Linda, Cay and me became firm friends over the next few years and it was with a great deal of pleasure that we watched Colin rise to become the Senior Naval Dentist with secondments all over the world. Now retired, Colin and family live in Australia where they built a very successful private practise in civilian life. Terrific people.

Flag Officer Plymouth's Band numbered some 35 musicians and buglers in total, so was small in comparison with my previous bands at Deal and Portsmouth. I already knew many of the band from previous times and I was looking forward to getting to know those who had been serving for years in the West Country bands. Plain sailing, surely? There was a lot of really good work happening within the band, but it was being spoilt by a few.

The first slight problem was that two of the buglers were currently in 'cells' (detention centre) for bad behaviour - I think drinking and fighting, although I do not fully remember the details of the case. This is a problem when you need four buglers at the front of the band and you are left with only two! The second problem, and much more serious, was a dysfunctional middle management in the band which had been at war for some time. My predecessor was aware of these tensions, but was hoping it would resolve itself without his intervention. The basic problem turned out to be the Drum Major, whose substantive rank was Corporal Bugler, being at odds with the Bandmaster who was a Warrant Officer 2, yet was allowing himself to be dominated by the Drum Major, three ranks his junior. This in turn caused problems with other SNCOs who were stuck in the middle of this power struggle. I knew I had to do something about this problem as it was a poison for the whole band. It was clear this had been festering for many months, so ignoring the situation was not going to be an option.

The third negative experience of this first week was HMS Raleigh Divisions (weekly parade) on the Friday afternoon. We had fielded the whole band to carry out the parade, albeit short of buglers (!). The parade went well enough, although the march-past at the end of the parade was the usual comedy of incompetent marching by the trainee sailors. When the parade was over I went back to my office to change out of uniform. Within a few minutes my telephone rang and the Commander (who I had met only once, briefly) spoke telling me the Captain (Captain Brian Brown (RIP) - later to become Admiral Sir Brian Brown, Second Sea Lord) would like to see me in his office immediately! Of course I knew this was not good news. I presented myself after a few minutes and was received by Captain Brown with great courtesy and coffee followed by questions about my new appointment. He was very interested in my hobbies and those of my wife and how I saw the next few years unfolding. I began to expect a 'recommend' heading my way regarding the parade. Wrong! Almost invisibly, Captain Brown changed tack and said, "and now to more weighty matters"!

He then outlined his view of the March-Past, which he saw the problem as the Band being out of step with the sailors - he was serious and I only just stopped myself from laughing in time! The next five minutes were awkward to say the least. My options were limited, as to argue with a Naval Captain was a bad tactic in my first week in his establishment, yet the only true answer was the reverse of what he was saying. I centred my comments around the fact that I had not served in a Naval Shore establishment before and needed to familiarise myself with the protocols that might be a little different from RM establishments. I reassured the Captain that I

John in the ITV Studios with Harry Secombe - early 1985
A young Phil Watson on the right. Years later Major Phil Watson - an excellent musician.
Next to Phil is Mark Petch (RIP) tragically murdered by the IRA at Deal in 1989

would meet with the drill staff and produce a recording of a March-Past so that the sailors could practise to a real-time rehearsal of the parade (which we did very thoroughly some weeks later). We parted on polite terms, albeit a little awkward. I eventually got on very well with Captain Brown, but not before I had made matters even worse a few weeks later!

Cay and I were hitting some golf balls on the 9-hole golf course that runs alongside the River Tamar in the HMS Raleigh estate. We saw someone walking their dog a long way down the fairway and, thinking we could not possibly hit the ball that far, I hit my shot. Of course the impossible happened, and my ball sailed through the air in the direction of the walker and hit the dog on the second bounce! Obviously concerned for the dog, and annoyed that the walker was walking where they shouldn't be, I hurried down the fairway to make sure all was well, and to tell the walker that they should keep their eyes peeled for golfers on a golf course. As I got closer I realised that the walker was indeed The Captain and he could probably walk anywhere he liked in his establishment. The conversation did not end well!

Lies, and Dammed Lies

My mind was finally cleared of any doubt as to how to handle the dysfunctional middle management over my first full weekend at HMS Raleigh when I was living in the Wardroom Mess before Cay joined me with our boys later that month. There were no band engagements scheduled for the band that weekend, so I had met with some old friends on the Saturday night for a few beers and catch up. In the early hours of Sunday morning I had a call from the Duty Officer in HMS Raleigh asking me whether we had a band working in Launceston the previous evening. I assured him that we didn't (because we didn't) and suggested that it might be a section of the band from CTCRM or BRNC band. I thought nothing more about this until later on the Sunday when I had another message left for me in the Wardroom to contact the Duty Officer as matter of some urgency. I was asked the same question about having a band in Launceston Police Club the previous evening. I assured him we didn't, but said I would double check with the Band Secretary and get back to him as this was my first week in the job and it was always possible that I could have missed something.

I contacted the Band Secretary (another old friend BdCSgt Steve Saunders[30]) who assured me that we did not have any engagements in Launceston that weekend so I conveyed this to the Duty Officer. I was left with an uneasy feeling when the Duty Officer informed me that both other bands had been contacted and they too denied any involvement at Launceston that weekend. I pressed the Duty Officer as to what the problem was and he informed me that a group of five Royal Marines musicians had been playing in Launceston Police Club as a Royal

---

[30] Steve looked after me as the DOM superbly well for the next four years four months. Steve and Rose became good friends of Cay and I. We enjoyed many a game of tennis together. The very model of a Band Secretary.

Marines Band. Not only that, but the band had stolen the patio furniture on departing after the gig!!

You can sense what was coming next.

On the Monday morning, after speaking to the Directors of the other two bands, I got the band together and asked the whole band was anyone working unofficially as a Royal Marines Band in Launceston Police Club on the Saturday evening. Nobody owned up. I then spoke with some of the senior members of the band who I knew well and asked them who in the band might go out as a Dance Band for such engagements? I was given a set of names. I got the suggested names into my office and asked them the question directly. They denied any involvement. This whole subject was now at Commander level in HMS Raleigh having been the central item in the Duty Log over the weekend, so I went to see the Commander to give him an update on the actions taken so far, and the result of my inquiries. Conversations had taken place at his level between BRNC and CTCRM and the general sense was that the culprits were from my band! We were beginning to look stupid.

I went back and interviewed the musicians again, who had clearly got together and decided that they best own up to this gig at Launceston Police Club in an unofficial (illegal) RM band capacity, although they still denied taking the patio furniture. They had blatantly lied to me several times, so the gloves were now off!

I instituted a search of the property of the most likely potential thief to check for patio furniture, and, lo and behold, there it was in his back garden!

The Musical Progress Cup, presented to Mark 'Taff' Jones (RIP) in 1986
L to R: Roger Waterfield, Barry Hill, John Perkins, Jeff Bishop, Dick Clarke, Taff Jones, Ken Peers, Steve Saunders.

To say this looked bad on the band is an understatement and, added to the other situations mentioned above, my course of action was now clear. Strangely enough, this unexpected turn of events, which characterised my first week in the job, set my leadership approach for the rest of my career, although I didn't recognise it as such at the time.

Anyone who lied to my face in similar situations received no support from me. Those who had the integrity and courage to admit their mistakes had my full support, insofar as it was possible, and legal!

A New Approach

I had hoped my first command would be a seamless join and I was looking forward to being 'Mr Nice-Guy' and having the musical opportunities that are available to the Director of Music. However, the fact was if the band was going to become the type of outfit I could be happy with, fundamental change had to take place. I knew this was going to be difficult and require a period of turbulence before things became settled. I was right; it took six months and required a replacement Bandmaster, Drum Major, a demotion of one of the JNCOs, and the introduction of a 'zero-tolerance' discipline culture. I had plenty of allies in the band such as my old friend The Band Secretary Colour Sergeant Steve Saunders, Sergeant Bugler John Tansey and Sergeant Terry Lane (RIP), Musician Robbie Coleman (the Librarian and '3-badge[31]' elder statesman of the band) to name a few, but I had to win some others over.

Another key moment

I started by giving the WO2 Bandmaster (who should have been all over this) another opportunity to put things right with regard to command problems with his SNCOs, particularly the Drum Major and general discipline in the band. I gave him almost five months as it turned out. Things came to a head in Guernsey in the October where he (The Bandmaster) was very keen to share some of the conducting with me. I agreed he should start the concert by conducting the National Anthem for the arrival of the Governor, then the opening sequence of marches after that. All very simple? The plan was, as the Governor entered the concert hall the timpani would play a drum roll, the band and audience would stand and the National Anthem would be played. I was standing in the foyer of the concert hall to welcome The Governor and direct him to his seat. What could possibly go wrong?

As the Governor's car approached I made ready for my part. To my horror I heard the sound of the timpani roll which carried on for some time, then the opening bars of the National Anthem.

---

[31] Meaning a musician who has three long-service badges.

The Governor was still in his car! To the reader this may seem like a small detail, but on Guernsey it was a major faux-pas, especially with this particular Governor who, being ex-RAF, was not a great fan anyway! By the time the Governor reached his seat the march sequence was well underway and I stood there, helpless, knowing that whatever we did for the next two hours would not smooth over the cock-up of the Anthem - and so it proved. I felt so sorry for Bert and Marge Dodsworth, lovely people, who were the organisers of this annual concert on behalf of the Charybdis Association. Bert and Marge had put so much effort into this weekend down the years and they continued to do so for many more. They soon became great friends and we were able to laugh at this inauspicious start, but for now it was damage limitation.

I know anyone can make a mistake, Lord knows I have made enough, but this was the last straw with The Bandmaster, so I resumed my lobbying of the Band Service Headquarters to have him replaced. We agreed that I could have my old friend Band Colour Sergeant Roger Waterfield as the acting Bandmaster in the interim. Roger and I were in training together and he was a completely different kettle of fish. Roger turned into an outstanding, much respected, no-nonsense Bandmaster. The Drum Major had also been replaced by the excellent Drum Major Keith Pullen and the band was more settled. Discipline was good and the band was playing well with some strong players amongst its number. We had a new build bandroom just agreed and I had managed to revise the plans to include a recording studio element. Now the game was on as far as I was concerned - almost seven months after I had arrived! Although I didn't know at the time, I would stay in this post for well over four years which gave me time to build something very special with the band.

The Official Opening of the new band room by Vice Admiral Robert Gerkin - 1987
John far left. Principal Director of Music Graham Hoskins 3rd from the right.

Welcome Additions

In 1985 the Commandos Forces Band, based at Stonehouse Barracks Plymouth, was disbanded and the personnel were sent equally to both CTCRM and HMS Raleigh. At a single stroke the numbers in the band increased by almost 25% and included some strong musicians such as Martin Dale, Trevor Brown, Henry Monaghan, George Tate, Brian Short, Reg Sheen and more. I already had some outstanding musicians such as Ken Peers and Gordon Carter (both of who went on to become the leading players in sound technology for the Band Service), Phil Watson and Tony Smallwood (both of whom later became DOMs and retired as Major Watson and Major Smallwood) and star players such as Eddy Gasser, Gary Pumford, Jon Camps and many other high calibre players. About the same time a young Nick Grace (later to become Lt Col PDM) joined the band straight from training as an 18-year old!

The band was becoming well known for musical excellence and we were being asked for ever more concerts around the country. At last we were punching above our weight. My relationship with Flag Officer Plymouth was very good and I served three different Flag Officers with equal success. Life in HMS Raleigh was also very good with its excellent sporting facilities and terrific support from the Staff. The opening of the new bandroom was the icing on the cake and we began with renewed energy using the new recording equipment that we had scrounged money to buy. In fact over the next two years we recorded 'Under The White Ensign' and 'The

Having abandoned Plymouth's Theatre Royal because of an IRA bomb threat, we took our instruments into the street and entertained the audience in an impromptu 'al fresco' concert. Richard 'Taff' Jones far right on piccolo would later be murdered by the IRA bombing of the barracks at Deal on 22nd September 1989.

108

John Perkins and Ken Peers editing 'The Plymouth Sound' LP.
'Old School' quarter-inch tape!

Plymouth Sound' albums which were engineered by Ken Peers and mastered at the Abbey Road Studios in London. At the same time we also attracted funding for an ongoing course in Sound Technology given in our Bandroom by David Ward the MD of the Gateway Recoding Studios based in Kingston polytechnic[32]. Apart from myself, the other main enthusiasts for the sound technology course were Ken Peers, Trevor Brown, Gordon Carter, John Beddow and Karl Westlake; all of whom played key roles in establishing the technical team that plays such a central role in all the major engagements undertaken by the modern Band Service. There was a tangible buzz in the band and I was loving it.

Cat. No: FOP1

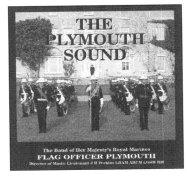

Cat. No: FOP2

Apart from the Charybdis weekend in Guernsey in October each year, the other fixed point was Flag Officer Plymouth's visit to the

---

[32] Sadly the course died when I left. However, not before much good had been done to stimulate interest and knowledge in key members of the band who progressed technological advances in the BS over the following two decades.

Liverpool area in May. The Band always played a full part in this weekend with Beating Retreat ceremonies and 'showing the flag' type engagements around the City. One year this included giving the opening concert of Royal Albert Dock on a floating pontoon in choppy conditions. Quite how the buglers managed to remain on their feet was testament to their fitness and agility! The main event in our eyes was the concert given each year in the Anglican Cathedral (England's largest) with the world-renowned resident organist Ian Tracey, and sometimes his Liverpool Philharmonic Choir[33]. This concert was a magnificent shop window for the Flag Officer Plymouth as he could invite all the key local dignitaries and provide a top-class entertainment for them whilst sitting and enjoying the concert himself. As Flag Officer Plymouth, the Naval artist Sir John Webster was full of praise for our efforts. Sir John sent for me on return to Plymouth and presented me with a watercolour painting he had made of the Cathedral the morning after the concert. The painting, which brings back many happy memories, hangs in our dining room in Deal.

A competitive racket sports scene with tennis, squash and badminton.
L to R: John Perkins, Dickie Darch, Terry Lane (RIP), Steve Saunders, John Brier

My time with The Flag Officer Plymouth's Band was certainly one of my career highlights. It was over four years in length which gave me time to build something exceptional, which those who served with me were proud to be part of. The musical reputation of the band was high and we became sought after for public concerts across the country. We were occasional guests of

[33] Some years later in 1995 Ian invited me to conduct the finale of Mahler's 2nd Symphony (orchestrated for concert band by John Hillier) with The Philharmonic Choir and my Plymouth Band. One of my stand out musical memories.

Harry Secombe and the 'Highway' Sunday evening ITV programme, and we had a strong relationship with the composer Ron Goodwin who became a regular visitor. In fact our solo clarinettist Musician Trevor Brown went on to transcribe many of Ron's film scores[34] for concert band with his unique magic touch. Some years later Trevor became the Staff Arranger for the Band Service producing some terrific concert pieces for band.

Our recordings had also made a mark and signalled a new way forward for recordings and sound technology generally. It also gave some of the younger members of the band an opportunity to showcase their ability and enhance their reputations. I particularly remember Musician Tony Smallwood (later to become Major Tony Smallwood) playing Gershwin's 'Rhapsody in Blue' in Plymouth Guildhall as an example. I wonder how many could emulate that today?

Sadly, our general success directly led to my two young flute players, Richard Jones and Mark Petch being selected (poached) to move to The Staff Band at Deal as their high calibre playing had been spotted. Within two years they had both been killed in the IRA bombing of the Staff Band on 22nd September 1989. They were so full of talent and fun. A cruel twist of fate.

Cay and I were sad to have to sell our house in Torpoint and make the move back to Deal in the summer of 1988. We had enjoyed the West Country and the friends we had made there. It was a different world away from the Headquarters at Deal and I wondered whether we would get another such opportunity. We had made a huge success of the FOP Band and it was time to pay the price. As Jim Mason told me once, "They will forgive your mistakes, but never your successes!" And so it proved!

The composer Ron Goodwin & Harry Secombe with
The FOP Band on Plymouth Hoe - 1984

[34] Such as Monte Carlo or Bust, Those Magnificent Men in Their Flying Machines etc.

CHAPTER 30

Compositions and Arrangements

I f the old saying 'that music is 10% inspiration and 90% perspiration' is true, then composition is that, and then some. For me, composition is hard work!

I started before the days of computers and notation programmes that have much reduced the man-hours involved in writing scores and instrumental parts. I always had an ambition to write music whether that was original composition or arranging music for various combinations of instruments. To that end I have spent a great deal of time learning about composition and orchestration and I have managed a few successes down the years. I suppose my first notable piece was an overture written in 1976 that I originally called 'The Viceroy' as it had a noble, if not heroic theme. In 1982 I reworked this piece and called it 'The Falklands Overture'. We recorded this overture in the Concert Hall at Deal with my old friend Phil Hughes conducting and me Leading an orchestra made up of professorial staff of the RMSM and members of the Staff Band. The purpose was to raise money for the South Atlantic Fund, which it did.

In 1981 my joint first study at the Royal Academy of Music was composition, reflecting my interests. Overall I would say that my experience in the mainstream of composition at the time was not inspirational, as the tide was very much in favour of 'experimental' music, more commonly described as 'squeaky door music'. I have never been drawn to 'contemporary art music' as, generally speaking, it does little for me. It gives me no pleasure to write or listen to[35]. I have heard pieces of contemporary music where I can appreciate the skill and craftmanship, but that is the exception. For me film composers such as John Williams are more to my taste, and an inspiration. Otherwise leave me in the 19th Century please!

The Falklands Overture EP

Thankfully I managed to find Malcolm McDonald as a tutor during my year on the Conductors' Course, so I spent as much time as I could with Malcolm and as little time as possible with the others. I produced a number of new works over this period which sadly were lost or thrown

---

[35] You can only say these things as you get older. It would have been sacrilege to voice this opinion during my time at The Royal Academy of Music - Emperor's new clothes etc.

away before seeing the light of day[36]. The only piece that remains from this time is my 'Elegy for Strings', which I still like and has been recorded and played occasionally.

Down the years I have had a number of commissions such as a march to commemorate the 45th Anniversary of D-Day ('The Dunkirk Veterans March') and 'March to The Palace' for a London based band. I have written the title track for a number of Albums including 'New Comrades', 'For Those in Peril on the Sea', 'Cole's Dream', 'The Ashokan Farewell' and very many arrangements for orchestra and band. I really have enjoyed writing, especially when getting fully immersed in a project. My only regret is not being able to get my music played as often as I would like, or at all in some cases! What is the point if nobody is playing it? It takes so much time and effort. However, I would not change a bit of it as you learn so much from the process, whether it is fruitful or not. So many (in fact most) of my fellow Directors of Music have not written a note of either compositions or arrangements. It takes courage to try and lay yourself open to criticism - which hurts. I know this from first-hand experience, but every now and again something magical and unexpected happens; ergo 'The Ashokan Farewell' (see The Plymouth Band later).

Conducting

I have always felt that good conductors are born with a natural talent to conduct and no amount of good teaching can make up for a lack of natural talent.

This is my view.

It is not to say that good teaching won't help because of course it will help you become the best you can, but you can spot those with very low natural conducting ability immediately - they always look as if they are working at it! Some are outstanding instrumentalists, but it doesn't necessarily transfer to conducting.

There are the stock answers in exams as to what makes a good conductor, generally starting with 'communication'. I would list confidence, clarity, good rhythm in your bones, personality, knowledge (especially score knowledge), keen aural sense, memory, believability and a knack to create a healthy tension during rehearsals (personality driven) as a fairly good list. Plus a certain 'Je ne sais quoi' for good measure. You need to reveal a lot more of yourself and your personality when conducting, much more than as a player, so it is a quantum leap to become an effective conductor.

---

[36] This includes my Serenade for 2 Horns and Strings, premiered at a Royal Academy of Music Concert. Sadly now lost!

I think there are also differences in conducting professionals rather than amateurs - different styles required for choirs rather than orchestras, from Brass Bands rather than Big Bands and so on. All these are real factors and need to be thought through, and often come down to your instinct.

The number of rehearsals available will be a factor. During my service career there was so much rehearsal time available it was lavish. It allowed time to dig into the detail of the music and create your own style. This never happened again for me when I left the RMs as everything was done at the rush on a tight budget.

Strangely, it is not always a good thing to have an abundance of rehearsal time unless you have something useful to say as a conductor. Time poorly spent can expose your lack of ideas, lack of aural sense and rehearsal technique, and lose the focus of the players. Too much talking can bore players. Boring rehearsals are a killer.

The majority of people I saw conducting in the Band Service had a lot of teaching, but were not really natural for conducting. They learned to do a job, but looked a touch awkward and had little useful to say. I guess they were in it for the career path, which is understandable and fine. The majority of people I have seen conducting in the civilian world have little or no aptitude for conducting either. This is often made worse by the fact that a high number of them have had no teaching as a conductor, so are basically just 'having a go' without any technique. Every now and then someone comes along and he/she 'is a natural' - hurrah (I refer to my earlier comments). Of course, there are as many different ways to be a good conductor as there are good conductors. There is no one right answer, but the universal truths are common to all.

In my last 20 years as a freelance conductor in the civilian world I have rarely had more than one three-hour rehearsal (less a 15-minute break) for a concert[37]. This means all you can really do is get through the music in order that we all know how we are going about the performance. All very frustrating and stressful at times. I became very impatient with people turning up late for the rehearsal or after the break as there was so little time, and none to waste. The same tardy people would want to finish not a second after the three-hour rehearsal slot!

Notwithstanding the negatives, if you enjoy the conducting process and the sensation of bringing the music to life, it can be the most rewarding of all the musical jobs. I loved it. If you are short on the skills mentioned above and it doesn't feel natural, stay away and leave conducting to someone else.

That's my view!

---

[37] The exceptions for me were when MD of an operatic society with weekly rehearsals.

CHAPTER 31

Supply Officer Music

After such an enjoyable, successful and productive four years with the Flag Officer Plymouth (FOP) Band it was my time for an Administrative job - normally a 2-year appointment. So started a period of four years three months where if it could go wrong, it generally did!

This appointment started well enough and I was made welcome by the incumbent PDM, Lt Col Graham Hoskins, who was close to retirement, and Lt Col Jonathan Thomson, former CO of the SBS during the Falklands War and rising star within the Corps. I was enthusiastic to do a good job as SO(M), but within a little over six months both of them had left and we had a new leadership team of Lt Col John Ware (PDM) and Lt Col Richard Dixon (Comdt).

I did precisely nothing musical with or for the Band Service throughout the whole of this long appointment, nothing at all! In more enlightened times the leadership always kept those in administrative jobs connected in some musical way to retain skills and interest for the future. I was kept away from any musical opportunities by the new PDM, who, I was told, appeared to see me as some form of musical threat. For much of this period, the leadership of Deal was unpredictable with both the Commandant and PDM occasionally at odds with each other; one coping with an alcohol dependancy (albeit a perfect gentleman, greatly liked by us all), the other an intelligent man, but uninspiring leader and PDM. The rest of us had to try to work and play around them - ask JH!

Add to this we had to sell our house in Cornwall and buy again in Deal, with no expectation of going back to Plymouth. We bought in Deal at the wrong time and sold the same house six years later for less than we bought it, having had to evict renters who eventually left owing several thousands of pounds and having trashed the house!

A major activity for the SO(M) at this time was as Editor of the Band Service Journal 'The Blue Band Magazine'. I enjoyed putting the magazine together from articles and letters sent in by readers and I also used the opportunity to sponsor two new books by the author John Trendell (RIP), 'A Life on The Ocean Wave'(The story of the RM Band Service) and 'Colonel Bogey to the Fore' (a biography of Major Ricketts *alias* Kenneth J Alford). This whole area was a learning curve as personal computers were in their infancy and the production process was changing from manual preparation to direct input into desktop computers. I enjoyed the artistic element of layout and design and I had terrific support from Alec Harwood, John Pring and Trevor Rowlinson who were all computer literate, ahead of the times. I also enjoyed working with John Felton (RIP)[38] at Adams printers Dover, who was my constant guide through the design and printing process.

Another key responsibility was to act as Sponsor Officer for The Royal Naval Volunteer Band Service which involved some inspection work and making sure suitable Volunteer Band Instructors (VBIs) were appointed to the thirteen Volunteer bands. I inspected the Volunteer Band in Gibraltar twice yearly - with golf clubs! My right-hand man for VBIs was WO1 Corps Bandmaster Roger Jones, a superb SNCO, travelling companion and all round 'good egg'. On retirement from the Band Service, Roger had a stellar second career as the Bandmaster at The Royal Hospital School Holbook in Suffolk.

Central to the Musical Supply Department was The Instrument Repair Shop, where six restoration technicians worked full-time to restore musical instruments and associated items. The repair shop was staffed mostly (5 from 6) by ex-RMBs who had learned the special skills of repair through experience in their playing life. They were larger than life characters and the atmosphere was lively, 'banter' being the order of the day - all day! John Wilkinson (strings), Terry Williams (woodwind), Tony Marsh (percussion), Doug Powell (brass), Joe Guest (brass) and Pete Rose (woodwind) completed the happy team. Before I left I managed to get their employment recognised as a 'Technical' grade within the Civil Service structure, which meant improved pay. It was long overdue and they deserved it.

Another vital area of Supply was the Central Music Library, which was the second largest music library in the country outside of the BBC. It comprised orchestral, wind band, marching band, fanfare music, songs, choral and original works. It also acted as a lending library. For a large part of my time The Chief Librarian was BdCSgt 'Riggo' Richardson, supported by Musician Mick Cole (RIP) who was severely injured in the IRA bombing. The civilian librarian was a highly qualified Librarian and violinist named Verity Steele who became the backbone of the whole system and transferred to Portsmouth with the organisation in 1996. Verity was a standout appointment who made a superb contribution to the organisation.

In the margins I was 'Positively Vetted' by The MOD as a Confidential Books Officer, and 'security' cleared to the level of 'Top Secret'.

The major upside to this time was getting together with three professors at the RMSM to form The Becker Quartet, named after Lew Becker, a former violin professor who had recently passed away. John Perkins (1st Violin), George Simpson (2nd Violin), Ivor Crocker (Viola) - later Jane Browne (viola), John Cullis (Cello) - much later Martin Thomas (cello). This kept me

---

[38] I would work on numerous printing projects with John in my second career post Band Service. A more gentle and kind soul it would be hard to meet.

sane and was the start of 25 years of chamber music concerts and events with The Becker Quartet/Orchestra, quite unconnected to the Band Service. This activity alone could be the subject of several chapters were there space. In fact I loved every minute of it and only finally gave this up aged 66 years.

The original Becker Quartet 1988

The Becker Quartet 1990 onwards

Project Officer

Throughout all this time I also acted as The Project Officer for the RMSM and worked long and hard on plans to move the RMSM to Portsmouth or elsewhere. I was also working with the Army on the Defence School of Music concept which to this day is still ongoing. I got along well with the Army PDM Lt Col Frank Renton, whom I had known from our time in Plymouth, but at the end of the day I was a Lieutenant and he was a Lieutenant Colonel who was always accompanied at meetings by another general list Lieutenant Colonel from the Army. None of our senior management attended these meetings with me. In truth there was very little enthusiasm for tri-service amalgamation at that time.

The only positive outcome to the many projects I was tasked with was the decision to recruit women into the Band Service, which was a recommendation of a study I had co-authored with Brigadier Malcolm Hunt - 'The Hunt Report' of 1991. We quickly established that approximately 80% of all youth orchestras were women and an increasing number of brass bands and youth wind bands were women, so it was inevitable that, to be able to recruit the numbers we required, this change had to be made.

During this time I had a strong team around me including my old friend BCSgt Ken Peers (an exceptional musician who I would work with in retirement) and Musician Trevor Rowlinson (a very smart guy and nice person who excelled with IT and administration) and we came up with many ideas, producing much detailed work for both relocation to Portsmouth and to redesign the estate at Deal[39]. The budget for the redevelopment of the Portsmouth project at one time, including a new concert hall, swimming pool and sports facilities, was approximately £17million. The whole process was thrown into disarray by the Deal bombing after which The Prime Minister, Mrs Thatcher, made a public announcement that Deal would not lose its Royal Marines. Obviously she meant well, but it just kicked the can down the road. There continued to be another six years of 'limbo' when the RMSM limped on in the barracks at Deal with raised perimeter walls and tons of razor wire.

In 1996 the RMSM eventually did move to Portsmouth on a shoestring budget of around £500K into the old Detention Quarters (Naval prison) in the Dockyard behind HMS Nelson.

John kept up daily practice on the violin throughout the whole of his career, unless it was totally impractical.

We knew the decision had already been taken in principle to close the Deal estate, thus saving large sums of money, and relocate the RMSM inside an existing Naval barracks in Portsmouth, most likely at that time HMS Excellent at Whale Island. I had been on the Whale Island planning team for some time precisely to achieve this. Because of an imminent announcement to close Deal, little or no money was being spent on maintenance and security of the barracks during the 1980s. Successive Commandants had been flagging this up as a security risk. We were a soft target for the IRA, as it proved in 1989.

---

[39] A great deal of detailed work had been done some years earlier by Captain Jim Rider and his team to produce a Defence School of Music model. Although a different proposal, this was helpful to our work.

CHAPTER 32

The Deal Bombing

The IRA Bombing of the Staff Band recreation space on the morning of 22nd September 1989 was one of the most cowardly and despicable acts of terrorism to take place on mainland Britain throughout the whole of the Northern Island troubles. The Commandant General of the Royal Marines, Lieutenant General Sir Martin Garrod appeared on national television condemning the bombers as "thugs, extortionists, torturers, murderers and cowards – the scum of the earth" and "We will emerge stronger and more determined than ever before to end and destroy this foul and dark force of evil". I totally agree with every word.

The previous evening of 21st September the Officers had been dining out Captain Ken Gill, The Admin Officer for the Deal Barracks. The Staff Band provided a small orchestra under the Direction of Band Colour Sergeant Jay O'Neill[40], another former Royal Yachtsman from my time in Britannia. As the evening's entertainments didn't finish until late the orchestra was given permission to come into work a little later the following morning. Had these musicians arrived for work at the usual time the number of casualties would have been even higher.

At the moment of the explosion I was getting out of my car on the parade ground in East Barracks. Everyone around sensed something big had happened and people were momentarily rooted to the spot wondering what had caused such a noise. I got back into my car and drove across to North Barracks via the Seafront and tried to enter Canada Road as the smoke and activity were pointing me to the area of the concert hall. Canada Road had already been blocked by uniformed Marshalls when I arrived, so I parked further down the seafront and hurried to the site of the bombing. On arrival at the scene, people who had arrived before me were doing what they could to recover casualties from the rubble. The emergency services were just starting to arrive. I realised that I was not particularly needed there and could be more useful setting up a control centre in the Main Administration building, so I headed to the PDM's outer office and teamed up with the Band Service Secretary WO2 (Bandmaster) Trevor Attwood to do just that. We knew that most of the key RM Officers/Administrators had left Deal for Scotland on the early train to go skiing, so the Adjutant, Training Officer and other senior management were missing. In fact, they would not hear about the bombing at all until later in the day when they started the long journey back to Deal. Inch-by-inch Trevor and I started to collate accurate information, establish lines of communication with other agencies and field the many telephone calls[41] from The Prime Minister and Prince Philip down. Others such as WO1 (Bandmaster &

---

[40] Jay was injured in the bomb blast having arrived for work at his regular time.

[41] It took time to get the telephone lines up and running as they had been temporally closed down because of the explosion.

RSM) Graham Harvey[42] and WO1 (Corps Bandmaster) Roger Jones and their teams were preparing the Sgts Mess to house the many family members and volunteers who were arriving from early on. It would be a few days before I came out of the barracks again to go home for a rest. It is worth noting the many acts of kindness from wives and volunteers that took place on the day. Everyone has their story to tell, and I know Cay sat for 10 hours with the family of one of those killed until the dreaded news was confirmed. Traumatic for everyone.

As Editor of the The Blue Band Magazine at the time, I had commissioned John Trendell to write a history of the The Royal Marines Band Service entitled 'A Life on The Ocean Wave'. At the point of publishing the book, which happened to coincide with the bombing, we jointly produced a postscript to outline the facts of that horrific day. We felt this was such a monumental tragedy to strike at the heart of the Band Service it should be documented in this new publication. Here is our account of the facts:

Friday 22nd September 1989

Excerpt from 'A Life on The Ocean Wave'

It was at 8.25am on the morning of this fateful day that members of the Staff Band of the Royal Marines School of Music were chatting, drinking coffee, and generally preparing themselves in the Recreation Room of North Barracks, Deal, prior to assembling on the parade ground for a rehearsal of the ceremonial presentations to be given during the following week at the Council of Europe complex in Strasbourg, France. Without any notice, a massive explosion occurred within the Recreation Room, the blast of which immediately blew out the walls, thus causing the solid concrete roof to fall within the building. Witnesses in the vicinity spoke of a "blinding flash followed by an ear-splitting blast". An immediate operation to rescue those within the ruined building was put into gear by RM personnel and the emergency services of the civil authority. The Junior Band were some of the first on the scene to help with the rescue as they were rehearsing on the main parade ground some 200 metres away from the explosion. Hospitals in the East Kent area were alerted to receive the many casualties, the most seriously injured being taken to hospitals at Canterbury and Dover, and less serious injured to Deal.

At first it was thought that the explosion had occurred in the nearby boiler house, but this suggestion was quickly ruled out. The Irish Republican Army subsequently admitted responsibility for planting a bomb in the barracks. It was revealed later in the day that ten members of the Staff Band had been killed by the explosion, with many more badly injured, including a civilian workman and block cleaner (who was an ex-bugler).

---

[42] It was a mystery to me why Graham was not commissioned as a Director of Music. He should have been in my view.

The Aftermath

As soon as the news of the atrocity was broadcast, expressions of sympathy and offers of assistance came in from all over the world. Visits to the injured in hospital were made in the days immediately following the outrage by HRH Prince Philip, the Captain General of the Royal Marines; Countess Mountbatten, the Archbishop of Canterbury, the Prime Minister and numerous retired and serving members of the Corps. Hundreds of floral tributes to the memory of those murdered were assembled at the entrance to South Barracks at Deal, one of which in the form of an anchor was laid by RM Commandos returning to Plymouth from an exercise in the Baltic; their landing craft was beached at Deal to allow the Marines to march to the barracks to pay their respects to their comrades.

Seven days after the explosion, on a sunny autumnal morning, the entire personnel of the RM School of Music, including Wrens and Naval Nursing Officers, marched through the crowded streets of Deal behind a depleted Staff Band, with blank spaces in the ranks acting as a grim reminder of the disaster. In words of the Principal Director of Music, Lieutenant Colonel John Ware, this march was an act of defiance to the evil men who had planted this bomb, therapeutic for the surviving members of the band, and a note of intent that the Royal Marines Band would continue doing that for which it is renowned. It also presented the townspeople of Deal with an opportunity to share in the grief of the Band Service, and to once again show their affection and admiration for their music-making neighbours. This march through Deal was broadcast on nationwide live television, and subsequently relayed to all parts of the world.

Police investigations made following the atrocity disclosed that two Irishmen had rented a holiday home in Campbell Road, Deal, several days before the explosion, the garden of which property abutted on to North Barracks. These men had indicated they were in Deal for a fishing holiday and had given false addresses to the owner of the house. Kent Police widely circulated a 'wanted' notice showing sketched impressions of the wanted men together with a woman accomplice. Almost a month after the explosion one of the badly injured musicians died in hospital, this bringing the total number of members of the Staff Band murdered by the IRA to eleven.

The culmination of the period of mourning came with the poignant, but impressive, Memorial Service held in Canterbury Cathedral on Wednesday 22nd November, the whole of which was broadcast nationwide on BBC Television. The service in memory of the eleven who died, and in thanksgiving for the survivors, and for the work of the rescue teams, was conducted by the Dean of Canterbury. The first lessons read by the Captain General, HRH Prince Philip, Duke of Edinburgh, and the second lesson by the First Sea Lord, Admiral Sir Julian Oswald. The Archbishop of Canterbury preached a powerful sermon and prayers were led by the Bishop of

Dover, the Chaplain of the Fleet, the Principal Roman Catholic Chaplain RN and the Principal Chaplains of Scotland and the Free Churches. During the service Lieutenant Keith Sivyer RM, Assistant Director of Music of the Staff Band, laid a wreath in Corps' colours superimposed with eleven white roses before the Nave Altar, and the names of those who died were read by the RSM of the School, WO1 (Bandmaster) Graham Harvey RM. The orchestra composed of members of the seven bands and Instructional staff at the RMSM, was led by Lieutenant John Perkins and conducted by Lieutenant Colonel John Ware. Music was played before, during and after the service, and particularly appropriate to the occasion was the rendition of the triumphant last movement of Beethoven's Fifth Symphony. During the laying of the wreath, the Band Service's own Dedication Fanfare "To Comrades Sleeping" was played by the Silver Trumpets of the RM School of Music conducted by the School Bandmaster, WO1 (Bandmaster) Roger Jones RM.

Memorial Service held in Canterbury Cathedral on Wednesday 22nd November 1989

The service was attended by members of the bereaved families, survivors, the Prime Minister, Mrs Margaret Thatcher MP; the Commandant General of the Royal Marines, Sir Martin Garrod; Governmental, Civic and Service Chiefs, and representatives of the emergency services, hospital and rescue teams. Every available seat in the Cathedral was occupied. Never before has the Band Service been the subject of such a cowardly attack, the implications of which have yet to be fully assessed. What is clear is that the resolve of the Band Service to continue has been demonstrated in the best traditions of the Corps, which is possibly the best tribute that can be paid to those who died. Members of the Band of HM Royal Marines, Royal Marines School of Music who died as a result of an IRA bomb attack at Deal - 22nd September 1989.

Musician Michael Ball
Band Corporal Andrew Cleatheroe
Band Corporal Trevor Davis
Musician Richard Fice
Musician Richard Jones
Band Corporal David McMillan
Musician Christopher Nolan
Band Corporal Deal Pavey
Musician Mark Petch
Musician Timothy Reeves
Musician Robert Simmonds

John briefing the Chief of Staff inside the gates of South Barracks.

Some years later, when retired, I became Chairman of the Deal Memorial Bandstand Trust, the aim of which is to keep the memory of the eleven who were murdered in Deal alive through an annual series of concerts on the Deal Memorial Bandstand. The highlight of the season each year is the visit of the Royal Marines Band which attracts audiences of 10,000 plus who want to be in Deal to pay their respects. I spent twelve years as Chairman of the Trust during which time we raised and spent £130K on improvements to the fabric of the structure and major improvements to the site and facilities. We also accrued a working fund of approximately £70K by the time I left the role in 2018. On retiring as Chairman at the RM Band Concert on 15th July 2018 I was awarded the Commandant General's Commendation[43] by The Commandant General himself (*see Appendix Four*). The Deal Memorial Bandstand is the most fitting memorial to those who were murdered on that fateful day.

Post bombing. I was left holding many of the difficult jobs after all around me had moved on. I was nominated as The Secretary of The Bombing Relief Fund, responsible for making recommendations of how to disperse the £1.2 Million in the fund. This was a big job and one that took two years of careful thought, sensitivity and imagination; setting up Trust Funds for Children of the deceased, reporting to the Trustees of the Fund (chaired by CGRM) and actioning decisions. I also acted as Families Officer to a number of bereaved families and just about any other job connected to the tragedy. My small team to account for the donations, banking and making recommendations to the 'working group' was Alec Harwood (ASO(M) at the time) and Trevor Rowlinson. Once we had draft proposals we presented these to a 'working group' comprising a range of all ranks at the RMSM before making firm proposals, which I

Seven days after the explosion the entire personnel of the RM School of Music marched through the crowded streets of Deal behind a depleted Staff Band, with blank spaces in the ranks acting as a grim reminder of the disaster.

then took to the MOD in London to present to the Trustees. All of our proposals were accepted by the Trustees and this large (and potentially contentious) fund was distributed and closed within two years without a criticism from any quarter. This was serious good work. I was delighted that my recommendation for The Commandant General's Commendation was approved for Alec Harwood and The British Empire Medal (BEM) was approved for Trevor Rowlinson. Thoroughly deserved.

---

[43] See Appendix 4

The Staff of SO(M) Department 1992
L to R: John Pring (ASO(M)), Les Barnes (Storeman), Lesley Woodcock (typist), Jayne Eley (Blue Band Subscription Secretary), Trevor Rowlinson (Blue Band Production), John Perkins (SO(M))

I was happy (indeed keen) to do this important work, but I was left doing it, mostly alone, long after others had moved on, and one person can only take so much. I too was struggling with the trauma of the whole thing.

Odds and Ends

During this time (1990 & 1991), my parents died within a year of each other which was very unexpected, both having enjoyed good health until their 70th year. Although long-retired from the RMs, my father was hit hard by the Deal bombing.

I also got myself banned from driving for one year for refusing to take a breath test (not failing a breath test - never have) in my own home having been followed by a police car as I approached my house. No accident or incident had taken place, I was simply following Cay (probably too close) who was in her car. We had exited our cars and gone indoors before the police car stopped outside our house and knocked on our door, insisting I take a test because my driving was a little erratic. I became indignant, believing it was my right to refuse, but the law had changed the previous year to allow the police to pursue into your house. My refusal - even in my own home - now carried a mandatory 1-year ban!

My run of negatives came to a head at the MFM 1992 when I was told by a good friend, who I believed was about to succeed me as SO(M), that he had been recommended by his Admiral to stay an extra year in his current employment which in turn meant that I too would have to stay in my situation for a 5th year or longer! I guess I cracked to a certain point at this stage and had a few beers (although I was not on duty) and was reported by the security team for being wobbly exiting the building. A more serious and further indignity was overhearing The PDM, effectively throwing me under the proverbial bus, reversing a proposed promotion for me in a telephone conversation with the Military Secretary two days later. All this took place within my earshot from a public telephone at the Abbey Road Studios where we were editing the MFM recording on the following Monday. Thanks a bunch!

The thoughts of retiring early had been in my mind for some time and the prospect of further time as SO(M) made this a solid plan, so I started looking for a civilian musical job that I could take. As a qualified Violin Teacher with numerous other diplomas, there were plenty of places to start.

It was only the intervention of the new Commandant of the RMSM, Lt Col Ian Gardiner, who was the only person to ask me what was going on in my life, that the direction of travel changed. Ian suggested (quite forcefully!) that I attend a 2-week course at RNH Haslar in Portsmouth under the guidance of Surgeon Captain Morgan O'Connell FRCPsych, a veteran of the Falklands war and an expert on 'burn-out' and psychological illnesses. I went to Portsmouth with Cay and the boys and used a married quarter for the two weeks. This was time well spent and I came back rejuvenated. I made the point to Ian Gardiner that I needed a musical job after such an unprecedented time in the margins, and within days I was offered Director of Music of the bands at The Commando Training Centre Royal Marines (CTCRM) or Scotland; I chose CTCRM.

The Staff of the Instrument Repair Shop 1992
L to R: John Wilkinson, Terry Williams, Tony Marsh, Doug Powell, Joe Guest, Pete Rose

Ian Gardiner had seen the quality of my work in projects and administration generally, and had even attended civilian concerts where I had been leading chamber groups, so he was very much on my side. His parting comment to me was something along the lines of, "John, you will be remembered as the finest PDM The Band Service never had". I took that as a compliment, although he was telling me, that having not picked up the proposed promotion to Captain, any aspirations of PDM were probably scuppered.

CHAPTER 33

The Commandos Band

What a contrast The Commando Training Centre (CTCRM) was after the dispiriting atmosphere of the Band Service Headquarters in Deal; a place in limbo with no meaningful ideas for a way forward post bombing. For me personally, The Band Service Headquarters was a negative place, whereas CTCRM was the opposite. I could not have been made more welcome on joining the band in September 1992. My predecessor Dave Cole had a good band going with lots of enthusiasm and talent at all ages. Dave and I had always got along well and never had a cross word in our service careers. I was sad when he was not selected for PDM. We remained good friends and collaborated on recordings with The Central Band of The Royal British Legion in retirement. Although we do things in a slightly different way, we both shared a passion for music which remained our common denominator and number one priority.

The handover was a brief affair as just one day after arriving at CTCRM, 26 of us left to fly to Singapore to join HMS Invincible for a 3-month deployment called 'Orient 92'. Just the tonic I needed to rejuvenate my passion for Band Service life.

HMS Invincible - Orient 92

Another old friend Clive Close was the WO2 Bandmaster and an excellent Bandmaster he was. Clive was unable to join me on Orient 92 because he stayed behind to attend a WO1 promotion board. He was replaced by another old friend and superb Bandmaster in Gary Pumford. Because HMS Invincible was short of accommodation in the PO's Mess (Sgt's Mess equivalent) we had made a request to the Commander to promote all the Band Sergeants to Band Colour Sergeants so they could live in the Chief Petty Officers' Mess. The Commander agreed, and so we set off with a band of 26 all ranks, including 1 x Lieutenant, 2 x Warrant Officers, 6 x Colour Sergeants and 2 corporals. A little top heavy by any standards, but everyone was happy with the arrangements, albeit very unconventional. My first big decision was to prioritise the equipment we were to take with us as space on the flight (three days in a Hercules Transport plane!) and space onboard HMS Invincible was an issue. Because seven of us were keen golfers I made golf clubs a priority and decided to leave the orchestral instruments behind to make room for them! I had heard worrying stories about the standard of orchestral playing in the band and thought, rightly as it turned out, that to perform as an orchestra would not show us in the best light. The next few months was just the tonic I needed and the trip was a huge success for the band and their multi talents. Socially they were a great bunch of people who got on well with the ship's company and took every opportunity to perform both in HMS Invincible and ashore for a wide variety of gigs.

The outward journey to Singapore was courtesy of an RAF Hercules transport aircraft with rope seats, minimal heating and certainly no cabin service! We had two stopovers for rest and refuelling in Brindisi, Italy and Columbo, Sri Lanka where serious runs ashore were had by all and then the final leg to Singapore. On arrival we found our way to HMS Invincible and went through the handover routine with WO(2) Bandmaster Simon Morgan and his CINC Fleet Band who had been onboard for the first three months of the deployment. We were to take over with an invisible join and jump straight into a full programme of events in and around Singapore before carrying on with the deployment. It really was a terrific band ranging from the elder statesman of Ken Schooley and Charlie Fleming (who had already served until pension, retired for a couple of years to civvy street, then rejoined) to a crop of 20-year-olds who were eager and talented. We made a good start onboard with everyone at all levels quickly integrating into their various messes and showing the positive attitude for which the band became famous. The exception was me!

The Orient 92 Band of 26 all ranks, including 1 x Lieutenant, 2 x Warrant Officers, 6 x Colour Sergeants and 2 corporals - never seen before or since!

Self-help needed

The CINC Fleet Band, under WO(2) Bandmaster Simon Morgan, had not included a Commissioned Officer in its ranks so I had to beg, steal or borrow a bunk in the Wardroom. This ended up in a cabin with three Harrier Jet pilots who, although charming, scary, yet wonderful, were closer to my son's age than mine and lived like students with their belongings strewn everywhere - especially 'trainers'! I lasted three days then I went into self-help mode. In the three days we had been onboard the Navy's largest warship I had searched high and low for a way around my dilemma. If nothing else I had realised that nobody was going to help me unless I helped myself, so my explorations took me away from the Wardroom Mess and around the working part of the ship.

I happened across a door on Deck 5 that read 'Admiral's Sea Duty Cabin' and was located alongside a row of operational rooms around the mid-ships on Deck 5. I cannot remember whether someone 'tipped me the wink' that this may have potential, but I managed to gain access to the cabin and discovered to my delight a veritable Oasis in the middle of the desert. The cabin had its own toilet, shower, storage and telephone as well as a desk and chair and comfortable bunk. I could hardly restrain my delight, but was brought back down to earth by my escort with the key who reminded me that this cabin was for the exclusive use of the task force commander (a Rear Admiral onboard who I had yet to meet) in case of operations/war, and that I would need to see the

John in Frock Coat Uniform - mid 80s

Commander (Executive Officer) of Invincible who might - and only might - pass the idea by the Admiral. Within minutes I was knocking at the Commander's door!

I had briefly met the Commander (Bruce Trentham) when coming onboard in Singapore and found him to be a formidable 'old school' no nonsense type of man. I made a mental note that we would get along just fine and so it proved over the next three months. My request to use the Admiral's cabin took him by surprise, albeit I had given him my sad tale of having to negotiate Harrier pilots' trainers and general clobber 24/7. He wanted no part of it and said words to the effect, 'If you want it bad enough, go and ask The Admiral'. Ten minutes later I was knocking on the Admiral's door!

Admiral Sir John Brigstocke KCB (he would rise to become Second Sea Lord) was a man greatly feared around the task group. He was not known for his sense of humour, neither was he long on conversation. As it happens he liked music and was keen to meet me as I had recently joined his Task Group. I presented myself as the newly joined Director of Music and we chatted about the band, its role, its personnel (and the high number of SNCOs I had brought with me!) and so on. When the conversation was drying up a little I broached the subject of my accommodation, explaining the current situation might be a problem going forward especially with ceremonial duties which were central to my work. I could see his interest drift away from my tale of woe and, when he stopped me he asked, 'and what do you propose to do about it?'

Yes, Yes, Yes, my opening - I dived in with, "I was wondering whether I might use your Sea Duty Cabin on 5 Deck all the time we are not at war or on operations?" An eery silence fell over the room. He paced up and down for what seemed an age. He looked at me a couple of times yet said nothing. I was almost at the point of saying 'forget it', when he turned to me and said, "YES". I thanked him for his time, left his cabin and set about moving my gypsy life into the Admiral's cabin that afternoon, a happy home for the next three months! Needless to say my stock had risen sharply within the Wardroom for having had the bare-faced cheek to ask the Admiral for such a thing - after all I was only a Lieutenant - albeit a Royal Marines Lieutenant!

Our happy band of Golfers

I personally liked Admiral Brigstocke and kept in touch with him and his son Tom on and off down the years.

On with the Tour

The next three months were filled with all the things Royal Marines bands do best, such as providing entertainment in Messes and in the Hangar for larger concerts and plenty of 'flag-waving' engagements ashore. All manner of hidden talents were discovered onboard to join in impromptu concerts. We had a few 'white knuckles' helicopter rides to play on the escort ships as well. The helicopter pilots loved nothing better than giving us a roller-coaster ride from one place to another especially when they were getting bored - but it was all great fun, the like of which would not happen in civilian life. After one helicopter ride I met up with the pilot in the Wardroom afterwards and we had some tea together. Apart from being in HMS Invincible as a Lieutenant Commander helicopter pilot, he was also wearing the red shoulder flashes of a Doctor. It transpired he was a fully qualified Doctor as well and he came from Canterbury, just down the road from me in Deal. Not only this, but he played the piano to Diploma standard which I discovered, as the days unfolded, was no exaggeration. He could also have been a professional musician! What a talent, and what a nice bloke. We played a few piano trios (Martin Sharp on cello) together on Sunday afternoons in the Wardroom, a little like a scene from an episode of Agatha Christie's 'Poirot!'

En route back to the UK we travelled through the Suez Canal stopping at Cairo, allowing the opportunity to visit the Pyramids, ride a camel and take in some of the nightlife. What a place, what a history, what a hangover!

John back on trumpet in 'Raffles' Hotel, Singapore, as a late substitute!

The next stop was Tel Aviv, the largest city in Israel. We had been scheduled to perform somewhere in the city which was the norm in a new port, but we were all taken aback by the arrival of an armed convoy to transport us. There may have been as many as 20 or so armed escorts with fully loaded weapons and a serious attitude who were to be our constant companions whilst we were ashore in Tel Aviv. One forgets the political climate that prevailed in this area in 1992. In truth we were slightly relieved to get out of Tel Aviv as the thought of a car bomb or the sound of gunfire was never far from our mind.

The next day we were taken by bus to Jerusalem for some sightseeing, a journey of a little over one hour across the desert. Jerusalem is about 40 miles east of the Mediterranean Sea. It is a hilly city with many valleys and is one of the oldest cities in the world that people have lived in continuously for almost 3000 years. It is important to three major religions. Jews consider Jerusalem a holy city because it was their religious and political centre during Biblical times and the place where the Temple of God stood. Christians consider Jerusalem holy because many events in the life of Jesus Christ took place there. Muslims believe that the Prophet Muhammad rose to heaven from there. Jerusalem has become a major cultural

The camel ride had to be done with my Indiana Jones hat

centre with over 70 institutions teaching the arts, some 60 museums, over 30 annual festivals, an annual marathon, 26 wineries, and over 1,500 public parks and gardens. All of these are visited by some 3.5 million tourists per year. This was without doubt the highlight of the trip in my view. So much history, sights and things to understand about this historic region. Growing up in a church-going family the biblical story was here all around us.

Our next stop was to be Cyprus from where we discovered that an RAF transport plane was flying back to the UK with plenty of space and could take the band. Given that the tour was done and the remaining ten days or so were to be spent sailing across the Mediterranean back into Portsmouth, we managed to get an early trip home courtesy of the RAF. For me this was

A memorable trip to the Pyramids

good, as I had yet to get into my main job at the Commandos Training Centre at Lympstone, Devon. What a trip and introduction to the new band!

Odds and Ends

It's funny the things that stay in your mind from certain trips, almost disproportionate to their importance. Whilst crossing the Indian Ocean towards the Suez Canal The Captain decided to stop at an uninhabited island in the middle of nowhere for some R & R. Beer and food was taken ashore and those who wished made their way ashore by boat routines to the sandy beaches. It was a much-needed change of scenery. I had a swim, a beer, something to eat and settled down for 40 winks on my towel, enjoying the warm sun. I must have dosed off because I awoke to the words, 'Hello John, fancy seeing you here'.

Waking suddenly, my vision had changed as the sun had been blocked out by my visitor and I looked up to see what I thought in my drowsy state was the composer Johannes Brahms looking down at me with his trademark long trailing beard and long black clothing (check page 125 of the Oxford Companion of Music, or google Brahms). For one fleeting moment I thought I had died and gone to heaven to meet all my musical heroes! Having shook myself awake, I realised that I was looking at the Reverend Charles Howard, Naval Chaplain and Chaplain at The RMSM Deal at the time of the bombing - what?! It transpired that Charles was on an escort ship for a short period of time and had wandered ashore like the rest of us. I should say that the weather was very hot, yet Charles was standing before me in all his Chaplain's black regalia, knee length coat, dog collar and top black hat. He always had the long flowing beard and facial resemblance to Brahms, but what a coincidence, what a shock. Of all the islands......... We repaired to the bar!

Preparing for a concert onboard

131

CHAPTER 34

CTCRM Lympstone Devon - The Commandos Band

On return to the UK I spent a couple of weeks at CTCRM before being drafted to RNC Greenwich as part of the RN Initial Staff Course. I was the only Royal Marine with 36 naval officers learning the finer points of Naval warfare from designing ships, naval tactics and all manner of lecturers and visits, including driving tanks on Salisbury Plain! Although I was woefully ill-prepared for the content of this course, I did pretty well overall and came near the top of the class. Subsequently I was recommended for the Senior Officers Staff Course, reserved for the future crop of senior leaders of the Royal Navy - how funny!

So it was after nearly six months I eventually joined CTCRM for 'real' and picked up the programme of events from Clive Close who had been doing a sterling job in my absence. I was sad that Clive was not commissioned as a Director of Music. He should have been, heaven knows I, and David Cole before me, gave Clive the most glowing of reports, but he was blocked at the highest level - and we could not convince those who called the shots at that time to change their minds. However, Clive served with great distinction at CTCRM and Portsmouth as the WO1 Bandmaster until he retired to become a schoolteacher. In quick time Clive's natural leadership talent was spotted and he became a Head Teacher and eventually an OFSTED Inspector. A good man!

Royal Naval College Greenwich 1993
Initial Staff Course - The only Royal Marine top right!

I enjoyed serving at CTCRM (Lympstone) where again the band enjoyed a good reputation within the Camp and the local community. We also had an exciting programme of band engagements including many concerts up and down the West Country and the occasional London engagement. The Military Concert Band was good and included some experienced leading players as well as a good crop of young talents who were improving all the time. The marching band was exceptional reflecting the amount of parade work undertaken in a new entry training establishment, and everyone took pride in their work. The least said about the standard of the orchestra the better! However, to be fair, this was not so unusual outside of Deal and Portsmouth where the orchestral requirement was minimal. There was also a strong culture of sports within the band, driven largely by the Sharp brothers (Martin, David and Joe) who were Corps golfers, fine footballers, and pretty useful at all other sports. Many others shared the love of sports and the band dominated sports competitions within the Camp. Andy Manley (The Colonel!) and badminton comes to mind.

I remember numerous excellent concerts during my time with the band including concert tours in the North of England organised by John Cooper (RIP) and Leicester Management. Great venues and well supported, these concerts raised the level of the concert band and 'Big Band' both of which were very deserving of the following they had. The annual concerts in the Colston Hall Bristol were highlights, normally combined with another band or guest conductor. Guest singers including Emma McParland who I would go on to make Big Band albums with at Abbey Road Studios some years later. Such was the standard of the playing that we put on a complete 'Big Band' concert in the Colston Hall which was no small achievement for a military band.

During my time at CTCRM we made two recordings, both recorded at Abbey Road Studios London. 'Marches of The Sea' and 'The Complete Marches of Kenneth Alford'. These recordings were in support of the RNLI (as were others in the years ahead) and Brian Williams, The Chairman of RNLI West Country Marketing, was a tower of strength in the whole process (*see Appendix two*).

Marches of the Sea *(A tribute to the Royal National Lifeboat Institution)*
The Band of HM Royal Marines CTCRM
Director of Music: Lieutenant John Perkins
Producer/Editor: Bob Whitney. Engineer: David Flower
Recorded at Abbey Road Studio 2
London - 22nd & 23rd June 1993

Fourteen of the marches recorded on this album are either composed or arranged by serving or retired Royal Marines. The idea for the recording was from the RNLI who wanted their newly

Cat. No: CLCD101

composed march 'The Lifeboatmen' recorded in their honour. The Lifeboatmen, the official march of the RNLI was written in 1992. It was commissioned by the Rame Peninsula Branch of the RNLI in memory of the late Sir Alec Rose, a passionate RNLI supporter. The march is dedicated to all past and present members of the RNLI. The composer, Trevor Brown, joined the Royal Marines Band Service in 1967 and served as a clarinettist in several bands, seeing active service in the Falklands Campaign of 1982. Trevor finished his career with the Corps as The Staff Arranger at the RMSM where his writing talents produced many successful compositions and arrangements for major occasions including The Mountbatten Festival of Music.

The Complete Marches of Kenneth Alford
(A Golden Jubilee tribute to 'The British March King')
The Band of HM Royal Marines CTCRM
Director of Music: Captain John Perkins LRAM ARCM LGSM RM
Producer/Editor: Bob Whitney. Engineers: David Flower, Alex Marcou.
Recorded at Abbey Road Studio 2, London - 18th & 19th October 1993

To make a modern digital recording of the Marches of Kenneth Alford was a project I had been keen to do as The Commandos Band was the direct successor of the original Plymouth Band based at Stonehouse Barracks where the legendary 'March King' Major Ricketts was the Director of Music many years earlier. The Commandos Band therefore wore the same unique cap badge awarded to the Plymouth Division Band in the early 1920s.

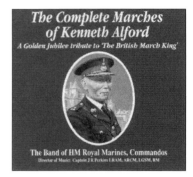

With the encouragement of Alford's biographer John Trendell, the support of the RNLI and to mark the 50th Anniversary of the late Major F J Ricketts retiring as Director of Music of the Plymouth Division, the time seemed perfect.

Cat. No: CLCD102

What struck me early on in the planning of this recording was the small number of marches in total Alford had produced over his lifetime, just 17 quick marches and 1 slow march. Always compared to John Phillip Sousa (The American March King) who wrote at least 136 quick marches, Alford's (The British March King) output was tiny. However, one cannot overestimate the quality and impact many of the compositions have to this day, and most all are instantly recognisable.

I spent some time talking to Harry Eden, who had been the flute/piccolo player in Alford's band, who recollected the hard taskmaster Alford had been as a conductor and leader. Harry in later life was the Professor of Flute at the RMSM and was an inspirational character to a whole generation of flautists during the 50s, 60, and 70s. Harry remembered well Alford's fondness for marches to be played in concert at a lively pace, 120 beats per minute or faster, and played with a more staccato style than was the fashion at the time. Those recordings made by Alford confirmed this and there was great energy and accuracy in the recordings I had listened to. In order to be true to this legacy I also recorded the marches closer to 120 beats than the traditional 116 beats per minute and chose a more staccato style which I too preferred. Others like Paul Neville described this more detached style as 'Band Style' - as opposed to orchestral style which generally followed a more 'full value' of the notes. We recorded the marches in the order they were written and included Alford's arrangements of both Lilliburlero and A Life on the Ocean Wave. As a contrasting epilogue to the recording I made a three-verse arrangement for band of Alford's Vesper Hymn, the pianoforte version (in manuscript) was found in Alford's papers when John Trendell was researching Alford's biography, 'Colonel Bogey to the Fore'.

I enjoyed the whole process of this recording and was particularly pleased to receive letters of appreciation from Alford's children who were in their eighties and delighted that such a tribute was made to their father.

Odds and Ends

The Normandy Landings 50th Anniversary

If there is one engagement that is both inspiring and humbling it is to be in France for one of the landmark anniversaries of the Second World War. I have been lucky to have been part of a number of these, but there is one particularly memorable year, for reasons both good, bad and lucky! This was in early June 1994 for the 50th Anniversary of the Normandy Landings.

The commemorations took place in a range of locations such as Pegasus Bridge, Bayeux Military Cemetery, Sainte Mere Eglise and towns and villages across the whole region. Finally the beach at Arromanches where The Queen would take the salute from thousands of veterans on the final day.

We had driven from Devon by coach with our instruments and equipment in our lorry. Our brief was to join an Army temporary camp under tents in the region and cover as many ceremonies and useful events we could find. No rehearsals, just make it up along the way. We had a couple of fixed points where Prince Charles was going to be and we had to be in support. On the last day we should present ourselves on the beach at Arromanches with our Army and RAF counterparts for the grand finale March-Past.

Our first slice of luck was the fine weather, which lasted for the three days we were in France in a field under tents. Our Army hosts were terrific and did all they could to make our ceremonial tasks easier by finding places to hang and clean uniforms for each new day.

The atmosphere in the whole region was buzzing with tens of thousands of WW2 Veterans milling around the bars and restaurants, and so pleased to see us turn up in uniform in their midst. It was impossible not to be inspired by their humility and their joy to be able to be there for these commemorations. After confirming all the locations for the VIP events, we decided to drive around the villages (which were throbbing with Vets) and put on a short entertainment every time we found a decent crowd.

On day two we had played for the main VIP event in the morning and set off on our wandering minstrel tour, eventually getting hopelessly lost in deepest Normandy having made a couple of random concert stops. It was now well after lunchtime so we decided to stop at the next town and find some lunch. On exiting the coach in the town square I noticed a throng of well-dressed people drinking and making merry in and around the 'Marie' so I wandered over (in uniform) to see whether we could attach ourselves to this party. The first person I bumped into was Lt Col Richard Dixon, formerly Commandant of the RMSM at the time of the bombing and my old boss and friend! Richard, now retired, was acting as a Tour Guide for Battlefield Tours and was one of the hosts of this party. What a chance encounter as we were hopelessly lost and very ready for lunch! Needless to say Richard made us all welcome and the free hospitality went down a treat. After reducing the French wine mountain we called it a day and found our way back to our tents!

The next day, the main event started in the early afternoon on the beach at Arromanches for a slow time rehearsal of the big March-Past. The three bands were formed up on the sandy beach with our backs to the sea. I think there was a guard of honour to 'Present Arms' on the arrival of The Queen, President Mitterrand, President Clinton and many others. After this, the march-past by the Veterans would commence from our right and continue along the sand in front of the VIPs who were stood on a saluting dais overlooking the beach. As it was impossible to get the Veterans to the beach for the rehearsal that part was taken as a given. Piece of cake I hear you say!

After the sketchy rehearsal we had a couple of hours to relax and change ready for the main event. We formed up as rehearsed some way down the beach facing the promenade and alternated playing incidental music with the Army and RAF bands. During this time the many thousands of veterans were being shepherded into marching groups further along the beach to our right. This was not the slick operation hoped for as many were elderly and some infirm, and all this was taking place on the sand, a surface ill-suited to marching. The schedule was slipping and the whole March-Past was getting delayed. I suppose the VIP party was being held back from the saluting dais until all was ready. OK; this is not a problem so far and certainly not a unique situation. However, when I turned around to conduct the band in our turn, I sensed a change to what was in front of me. The tide was coming in - and fast!

No doubt the organisers had taken into account the beach conditions and tide, but they clearly hadn't factored in a delay now approaching an hour or so. As luck would have it about this same time the March-Past was ready to start, so the Parade Commander gave the order for the Guard to 'Present Arms', we played the National Anthem and the long lines of Veterans (thousands of them) started their March-Past. I was conducting the band and facing the sea witnessing the water gradually seeping up through the sand as it made its relentless progress up the beach. First the clarinets, then cornets, horns and finally trombones and basses fell victim to the sinking sands. It was so funny really, but it was such an important occasion being televised around the world that it could have ended up a National embarrassment.

At the very last critical moment we had our chance to step off and advance up the beach. The heavy instruments took the greatest toll and weighed the players down into the watery sand which was now over our feet making it hard to step off. We must have looked comical, but fortunately the attention of the world was focused on The Queen and VIP party, so, by the time we extracted ourselves, we managed to gain some composure and complete the event in style. Another five minutes in the wet sand and I am sure the event would have gone down as one of the biggest peacetime fiascos of all time!

Heading further West once again

All in all the CTCRM Band was a joy to be part of and I would have happily spent more time there, but after almost 10 years as a Lieutenant, I was promoted to Captain and appointed Director of Music of the Plymouth Band, now a Staff Band based in HMS Raleigh, my old stomping ground.

If CTCRM was a terrific appointment, the possibilities in the new Staff Band at Plymouth were even more exciting. I couldn't wait to get there, especially as this time Cay and the boys were able to join me as we had been allocated a married Quarter just outside the gates of HMS Raleigh. I had spent the previous two years commuting from Lympstone to Deal at the weekend whenever possible. The journey was difficult to say the least and living in the Officers' Mess in your mid-forties when all around you were in their early twenties had limited appeal! So, on 24th July 1994 I joined HMS Raleigh once again as Director of Music of the newly enhanced sized Staff Band of HM Royal Marines Plymouth.

In Egypt 1992

CHAPTER 35

The Plymouth Band

I t's funny how things even out over the years. I hadn't expected to serve at HMS Raleigh again having had over four excellent years there between 1984 - 1988, but the reorganisation of the Band Service that upgraded The Plymouth Band to one of the two major Staff Bands presented me with another unexpected opportunity. The band was full of many old friends and some excellent musicians amongst them. I was able to cajole a few other key 'star' players to come and join me, courtesy of the Drafting Officer, my old friend, run ashore oppo, best man, and good egg Lieutenant John Hillier. John also sent me most of the 'draft' margin[44] extras which had the combined effect of temporarily raising the overall numbers of the band to around 88 all ranks. Unbeknown to any of us at the time this had a profound and lasting benefit for the Band Service as one of my first tasks was to meet with Naval architects to explore the possibility of extending the Band facilities to accommodate the new sized band. When calculating new building there is a Joint Service Publication called 'JSP101' which is the bible. Along with everything else it lays down the space, in detailed meterage, for band accommodation, both musical and administrative. The key is that it is based on the numbers of people to be housed within the new build.

Another New Bandroom

My first meeting with the architect, who luckily was a fan of Royal Marines bands, laid out the basics for the new plan. It was clear from the start that he looked forward to this job and was keen to do as much for us as possible. One of the first questions he asked was, "How many are in the band?" I was able to answer honestly 88 all ranks, which was true[45] albeit a massive distortion of the real 'entitled' complement of around 50 all ranks! Believe it or not I was never directly asked this question again and the whole project proceeded on the basis of 88 all ranks. In effect the overall build was now almost twice the size of our true entitlement. Not only that, but I managed to persuade our friendly architect to include a consultant acoustician to be part of the planning and incorporate a recording studio of professional specification into the design. The project was moving ahead at great pace and initial funding of around £1.2M was agreed mostly through an old friend from CTCRM Major John Spencer who was now overseeing RM Building projects. This whole exercise had been conducted without any input from the Band

---

[44] Spare players who were over the normal complement of bands, yet who were necessary to cover shortages should they occur. At the time there was an exceptionally large draft margin because a redundancy tranche had been instigated to cater for the reorganisation of the bands and the move of the RMSM to Portsmouth. The bands reorganised early which left extra people surplus to the new requirements.

[45] To the best of my recollection all these years later.

Service Headquarters who were preoccupied in moving from Deal to Portsmouth. As it turned out the project expanded as it went along, resulting in an overall cost of over £2M, the excess being met from within the Plymouth (Naval) Command. Within nine months of me joining the band we had vacated the old band accommodation[46] and moved into the empty Wrens New Entry Block whilst work was underway on our majestic new build. To put this in perspective, at the same time, the RMSM at Deal was moving all training/Headquarters and Supply and support activities to Portsmouth with a total budget of £500K!

It took a little over 15 months to complete the new build and, believe it or not, I was drafted to Portsmouth a couple of weeks before the official opening (to which I wasn't invited) by Prince Philip. I believe I was not forgiven for going my own way with this project, and I was certainly not going to be given any formal credit for the undisputed success of the project. Again, no good deed goes unpunished! I didn't mind really as I had a wonderful two years with this outstanding band and nobody could take that away.

To this day the Plymouth Bandroom is the best of its kind in the country. Down the years many of the new generation in the Band Service have gone out of their way to thank me for the effort (and cunning!) I put into attracting the finances and getting this facility built to such a high specification. They say it would not have happened to such a standard without me; and they are right!

Tragically, before any of the above work began, disaster struck the band in the form of a road traffic accident which saw Musician Barry Holland killed and many badly injured.

---

[46] The build of which I had overseen during my first tour as Director of Music in HMS Raleigh in 1984 - 1988.

CHAPTER 36

The Band Coach Accident - 18th September 1994

It was a sunny Sunday afternoon in September, what you might call perfect Autumn weather, when the disaster struck. We had been tasked to provide a large sized band to support a major event on Horseguards Parade London and had been joined by a number of Musicians and Buglers from The Band of HM Royal Marines Dartmouth in order to field a suitably impressive size band for a major London ceremonial engagement. We travelled the day before and stayed overnight to be in position for the engagement on the Sunday morning. The parade, on a beautiful sunny day, was uneventful and everything went as planned, finishing a little before midday. On completion, we changed into civilian clothes, packed the coach for the return trip and dispersed for an hour into the local area to get a drink and bite to eat before the 4-hour return trip to HMS Raleigh.

I believe we left London around 2pm and set off down the M4/M5 route back to Plymouth. The driving conditions were perfect, being clear and sunny the whole time. We stopped at Bristol Services for a break for the driver, then onwards down the M5. Traffic was normal for a Sunday afternoon and we were making good progress. Our coach was a double-decker type with tables and chairs downstairs and rows of paired seats upstairs. I remember chatting to my SNCOs (Gary Pumford, Pip Shell, Barry Hill, Steve Muddiman amongst others) who were mostly downstairs with me, some of whom were facing forwards in the direction of the traffic and some facing towards the rear of the coach on the reverse side of the tables. We had only been on the M5 for 20 minutes or so when we came over the brow of a hill and down the other side. Those of us facing forwards could see quite clearly that there was a traffic jam half a mile or so ahead, and that the traffic was stationary. Unfortunately the driver just saw traffic and assumed it was moving as the two sights can look shockingly similar on motorways. There is no doubt in my mind (although I cannot prove it) that we were travelling too fast in the outside lane of a three-lane motorway. By the time the driver realised that the traffic in front was static it was much too late.

Those of us who could see what was about to happen were screaming as loud as we could for the driver to stop, but he didn't get it and carried on at speed only realising seconds before impact. He swerved the coach to the left clipping the end of a mini car and careering off the motorway in a series of rolling summersaults down the embankment, and eventually coming to rest upside down in the adjoining field. We were thrown around inside this 'tin-can' like pinballs. It was terrifying. When we were able to move, those that could forced their way out via windows helping those who were more seriously injured into the field alongside the coach. Members of the public in the traffic jam on the motorway started to appear and help, and the situation was slowly organised with the seriously injured lying clear of the coach in the field and the walking wounded (of which I was one, not being able to raise my left arm and cut and bruised) were doing what they could for others.

In the middle of this chaos, I remember asking the Drum Major Steve Muddiman (a superb SNCO and Drum Major who I liked enormously) to find his nominal list of everyone we had onboard and start an inventory of who was OK, injured or worse. The coach was upside-down in a ditch with the front end submerged in the muddy ground, so it was not clear whether everyone was out of the vehicle. About this time I remember emergency vehicles turning up and fire brigade officers were inspecting the coach. After a few moments, as the Officer in charge, I was asked to join the Fire Chief who said he would like me to crawl into the coach with him as there was a fatality inside who needed to be identified before they could proceed further with their work. This I did, and I had the sad duty of identifying Musician Barry Holland as the fatality.

There in itself was one of the most horrible coincidences of my service career, as one of the musicians who had joined us from The Dartmouth Band was Barry's brother Terry, and they were sitting together on the coach on this fateful day. I had known Terry from the Deal bombing as he was one of the very seriously injured in that bombing, and it was a miracle he survived. His parents were lovely people, so immensely proud of their two boys and I could not imagine how they could cope with this tragedy. Cay and I kept in touch with them for a number of years afterwards and a more impressive couple it would be hard to describe. I think they too thought it a miracle that Terry walked away from this day unscathed. Terry now works as a civilian store-man for the Band Service in the Supply Officer Music's department in Portsmouth. What commitment to the Band Service.

When one considers the many thousands of miles travelled by bands in coaches each year it is hardly surprising that there have been a few close encounters with disasters. You could say, and many have, that this was an accident waiting to happen, but there was no good reason for it. Driving conditions were perfect. It was in the middle of the day when nobody, least of all the driver, should be tired. Given that it did happen and how dramatic the crash was, we were very lucky that there were no further fatalities, albeit many had some horrid injuries. The fact that it was daylight, dry, and relatively close to the major regional centre and hospital of Bristol certainly helped with the work of the emergency services.

I think it is fair to say that this terrible incident changed the way many of us (myself very much included) viewed travel by road and especially coach. I am sure it was a major factor in one or two of our number deciding to call it a day and leave the Band Service earlier than otherwise they might have. I know I have never slept on a coach from that day to this and I am a nervy passenger in all forms of transport. It was some months before I could drive again, but eventually I got back to it and today prefer being the driver myself rather than being driven.

The band had a major public concert the following weekend in The Pavilons in Plymouth. It was decided amongst ourselves that it should go ahead and all those that were able should take part. It was a therapeutic exercise and we dedicated the concert to our lost colleague Barry Holland. It was an emotional night that we all remember clearly. Barry's funeral was held in HMS Raleigh and was packed with Barry's family and many friends. Representatives from other bands were present together with the Commandant and Principal Director of Music from the Band Service Headquarters. The band played beautifully and Barry was given a terrific send off. So sad.

Odds and Ends

Like everything in the Band Service, humour is ever-present and I have one lasting memory of visiting the injured in Bristol Hospital with the Commandant General (The head of the Corps of Royal Marines) some days after the crash. I accompanied the General from bed to bed and introduced each of the injured. On arriving at Musician Andy Clarkson's bed, Andy stiffened himself to the position of 'Attention' whilst lying down, and made an attempt at a salute for the General! So funny! We could all sense there was more to come, and the General picked up on Andy as a bit of a character, so engaged him in conversation. Andy was in his mid forties at this time so was an old hand, not intimidated by senior officers. After some chit-chat the General asked Andy, "What is your proudest moment in the Band Service?" Andy replied, "When my son, who joined the Corps a few years ago, became senior to me." The General inquired, "And what rank is he?" Andy shot back, "A candidate for promotion sir!" Others could overhear this conversation and there was much laughter, although Andy remained deadly serious. I had known Andy since we were boys in 1965 and this was par for the course. What a great character and stalwart of the Plymouth Band. To see him 'breakdancing' was a sight to last a lifetime and we traded much banter in the course of rehearsals and life on the road. I liked him a great deal, but I never let him know that! He christened me 'the smiling assassin'. A little harsh I thought!

CHAPTER 37

Band Secretaries

T he job of the Band Secretary is pivotal to the success and smooth running of the band and life in general within the establishment. I was especially lucky to have BCSgt Steve Saunders doing this job for me during two tours in HMS Raleigh as the DOM. A quiet and conscientious man who had found his niche in life. Tenacious and loyal to a fault (not only with me, but my fellow DOMs), Steve was the very model of the perfect supportive Band Secretary, not a bad tennis player either! The Band Service had a knack of finding these special characters from within its number and another giant in this area was BCSgt Neil Evans in The Portsmouth Band. Neil had good instincts for all aspects of the job and shared the same high qualities of tenacity, commitment and man-management, working long hours to ensure a seamless programme of events for the band on 'the road'. Others in the same mould who were terrific during my time with various bands were BCSgt Mike Reynolds at CTCRM, BdSgt Neil Silvester at RMSM and Sgt Bug Lee Hodges who went on to an outstanding career in a sequence of administrative roles.

I am immensely grateful to them all.

The Martial Music of Sir Vivian Dunn
The Band of HM Royal Marines Plymouth
Director of Music: Captain John Perkins LRAM ARCM LGSM RM
Producer/Editor: Bob Whitney. Engineers: David Flower, Guy Massey.
Recorded at Abbey Road Studio 2, London - 18th & 19th October 1994

The first recording I made with the newly enhanced Plymouth Band was in October 1994. I was convinced that making recordings was the one certain way of raising the standard of the band, not least because musicians have a great sense of personal pride in their work and focus like no other time when in a recording studio. I had known this with certainty since my time ten years earlier with the Flag Officer Plymouth's Band and making our own recordings. Many years before that I had been involved as a trumpet player making recordings from the late 1960s through to a series of recordings in the mid 70s in Abbey Road Studios with Paul Neville who shared this same view. It was

Cat. No: CLCD10394

a reason for detailed rehearsals and the reinforcement of good habits, so the next recording was always on my mind.

I had been planning for some years to make a complete recording of the military music of Sir Vivian Dunn (FVD), much of which was played by RM bands on a weekly basis. My connection with Sir Vivian went back to my childhood when my father was in his band and played all kinds of other 'non-musical' roles for FVD, including making horseradish sauce, cutting his hair and for some years the concert hall caretaker. Titles such as, 'The Captain General', 'Globe and Laurel', 'Soldiers of the Sea' and 'Cockleshell Heroes' had obvious Royal Marines themes and, during Sir Vivian's long service in the RM Band Service (retiring at the age of 60), his new compositions had become a regular and central feature of our repertoire. Like his illustrious predecessor, Major Ricketts (alias Kenneth Alford), FVD had the knack of producing inspirational and memorable marches which combined catchy tunes, harmonies and rhythms to lift the spirits and inspire marching men and women. Indeed they went further as both composers developed a style of composition that became instantly recognisable as the Royal Marines sound.

I had kept in touch with FVD down the years and at the time of recording this new album our two boys Nicholas and Stephen were studying at Ardingly College, a boarding school only three miles from FVD's home in Lindfield, West Sussex. FVD had taken the boys out for Sunday lunch when we were unable to collect them for the weekend. They remember a terrifying drive from the school to 'The Bent Arms' in Lindfield, which was FVD's favoured pub/restaurant. The memory of FVD driving like a maniac with a cigarette in his mouth with the ash falling randomly down his shirt, tie and waistcoat stays with the boys to this day! Sir Vivian was very kind to our boys and we appreciated his generosity.

FVD's music was produced before the days of computers and all original compositions were written by hand and copied by librarians onto 'march-cards'[47], a specialised skill necessary to fit all the musical content on one side of the march card, yet still be legible. Gradually some of FVD's marches were printed professionally by the publisher Boosey and Hawkes which gave them wider circulation and easy access around the world. Even so, the combined published and unpublished martial works[48] numbered just 21, including arrangements of other tunes such as 'Famous Songs of the British Isles', 'Westering Home', and 'Where e'er you Walk'. A low total number as it appeared we were always playing FVD marches. To add further interest and information for the listener I asked my friend and military historian John Trendall to write the CD booklet notes to accompany the recording. We recorded the album in Abbey Road Studios on 18th & 19th October 1994 and the recording was released later that year. The Dunn family were thrilled with the result and very humbled that we had gone to so much trouble in

---

[47] Rectangular cards of small size that could be held in the music Lyre that attached to instruments allowing the musician to march and play the music with ease.

[48] FVD also produced very many orchestral and other misc works for band, most notably fanfares of high quality.

researching and recording this important collection of military repertoire; it had never been done before or since. Paddy Dunn (FVD's son) told me how much this whole project meant to FVD who at this time was terminally ill.

For Those in Peril on the Sea

The Band of HM Royal Marines Plymouth
Director of Music: Captain John Perkins LRAM ARCM LGSM RM
Producer/Editor: Bob Whitney. Engineers: David Flower, Guy Massey.
Recorded at Abbey Road Studio 2, London - 19th & 20th October 1994

Another recording made at the same time as 'The Martial Music of Sir Vivian Dunn' was 'For Those in Peril on the Sea', a collection of maritime music dedicated to the RNLI. This companion album to 'Marches of the Sea' was another collaboration with Brian Williams and his RNLI West Country Group who helped to fund the project. All our recordings served to boost RNLI funds over the years ahead and cement our relationship with the Institution.

Cat. No: CLCD10495

For me, I had enjoyed these recordings, yet I believed we could play with more flair and style given a little more time together. And so it proved.

Shortly after this project was released The Plymouth Band was tasked to support a festival in the USA early in 1995. This meant getting out there to plan the trip with my Drum Major to decide what we could do best to support the event. So quite by chance, the story of 'The Ashokan Farewell' was born.

CHAPTER 38

The Ashokan Farewell
The Band of HM Royal Marines Plymouth
Director of Music: Captain John Perkins LRAM ARCM LGSM RM
Producer/Editor: Bob Whitney. Engineers: David Flower, Douglas Blair.
Recorded at Abbey Road Studio 2, London - June 1995

My variations on The Ashokan Farewell (in a classical style) was made one evening in our house in Torpoint Cornwall in 1995 over a two-hour period. Once it was finished that evening, I never changed one note or revised it in any way, yet this simple piece of work, which came to me so easily that day, has captured the imagination of millions of listeners around the world since we made the recording in Abbey Road Studio 2 in the Spring of 1995. It has remained in the top 60 of the Classic FM Hall of Fame since 1997 (its highest position was 3rd in the chart in 2003) and has sold more than one million copies in all formats to date[49].

Cat. No: CLCD10595

The idea for the arrangement came in 1995 when The Plymouth Band was invited to take part in the Azalea Festival held in Norfolk, Virginia, USA. Music associated with the Civil War (1861-1865) had come to my notice on a 1-week recce visit to Norfolk I undertook with my Drum Major Steve Muddiman a few months before the main trip. I heard this haunting tune (played as a solo folk fiddle) as part of the musical backdrop to the Civil War television series shown during our visit so I jotted the main theme down, thinking I may arrange this for the band later. This I did[50] on return to HMS Raleigh, playing the arrangement on the first occasion in the Roebuck Theatre in HMS Raleigh at one of our regular series of concerts. I remember coming off stage and Mark Searle (our excellent pianist) was in the changing room. Mark said words to the effect of, "You will be remembered for this piece long after you have left The Band Service". How prophetic. We prepared the new piece as part of our concert in a large concert hall in Norfolk USA. The concert hall was packed with well over 1000 people and we saved The Ashokan Farewell until towards the end of our show. I left the stage as the conductor and came back on with my violin and went into the new arrangement. The effect was stunning with people standing and applauding and many of the audience visibly moved by the performance. Although this was meant to be a 'one-off' performance, I quickly realised that we had to do something more with this when we returned to the UK, and the idea of an album of solo items,

---

[49] Including digital downloads and compilations.

[50] Having got permission from the copyright holder for the sum of £25!

146

of which this would be one, started to take shape in my mind. Given this had never been done before by a military band, it was a risk and did not receive enthusiastic support from all quarters.

I was confident that I could bring this project off as I had some of the finest players in the Band Service in the Plymouth Band at that time, many very capable soloists in their own right. Principal woodwind players included Michael Miller (Clarinet), Barry Hill (Oboe), Pip Shell (Flute), Jon Ridley (Bassoon - years later Lt Col Jon Ridley PDM RM). Ivan Hutchinson (Trumpet, and now The Corps Bandmaster) and Martin Dale (Saxophone) would be first choice soloists at any time, so we were tripping over ourselves with options. The silky relaxed style of playing had become the style of the band and we had rich talent in depth in every section, including the likes of Richie Fenwick, Jon Camps[51], Gav MacFarlane, Colin Hudson, George Tate, Mark Philips, Stu Bilverstone, Darren Smith, John Moss, Joe Reekie, Gordon Carter, Dean Waller and plenty more superb players. I constantly encouraged leading players to play in a more soloistic orchestral way and it was becoming second nature to do this. There was a sense that we were ready for just about anything.

The Ashokan Farewell Soloists
L to R: Barry Hill, Pip Shell, Dusty Miller, Jan Dale, John Perkins, Mat Harding, 'Grandad' Johnson, Ivan Hutchinson, Gavin Clemons

Besides arranging 'The Ashokan Farewell' for the album I also arranged 'Träumerei' by Schumann and Bach Sonata No 4 in C BWV 1033 for our Principal flautist 'Pip' Shell, and 'The

[51] Jon is a superb all-round musician who became an excellent conductor. He helped arrange a series of lunchtime concerts in HMS Raleigh where we introduced many new symphonic wind band pieces.

Swan by Saint-Saëns for our terrific Euphonium player David (Grandad) Johnson[52]. There was much to do before our two days of recording in Studio 2, Abbey Road Studios, London. I also persuaded the composer Gordon Langford (RIP) to 'tweak' his 'Rhapsody for Trombone' (originally written for Don Lusher[53]) adding a harp part and other little touches for our trombone soloist Gavin Clemons. I took Gavin to Gordon's house in Seaton, Devon for some personal coaching by the composer. What a gent Gordon was at all times. A model professional.

We made the recording in Abbey Road Studio 2 with my old friend Bob Whitney producing and mastering the album and David Flower engineering. Again, John Trendell produced the programme notes for the booklet. The whole project was beautifully done and we were rightly proud of the result. In fact I would go as far as to say this was a model project for any Director of Music, being original in its concept, well planned and executed, requiring skills of conducting and rehearsing, arranging some of the music and performing as the soloist on the title track. All the things I had been trained to do down the years.

However, the event that changed its fortunes was The Mountbatten Festival of Music in London's Royal Albert Hall in the Spring of 1996 when I performed The Ashokan Farewell with the Massed Bands of the Royal Marines over three nights. The concert was attended by Sir Paul Condon, a former Commissioner of the Metropolitan Police, who subsequently had our recording as one of his Desert Island Discs on the popular BBC Radio Two programme. At a stroke the recording reached millions of listeners and the rest is history. An old friend Richard Baker (RIP) also played this on his BBC Radio Two programme and Classic FM, not to be outdone, took our recording up and it quickly became the most requested recording on Classic FM too, much thanks to Jane Jones.

I have played the piece all over the country in major concert halls as well as many smaller events and many funerals! The most notable performance I gave was in 2001 with The Royal Philharmonic Orchestra in a packed London's Royal Albert Hall which was broadcast live on Classic FM. An exciting experience (if not a little daunting!) made more so as there was barely time to rehearse the piece. Our good friends Jane Cullis and Jane Browne joined my wife Cay to support me in the audience, and a good time was had by all! I left thinking, 'did that really happen?'

---

[52] 'Grandad' Johnson had a huge musical talent and he became a first class conductor and arranger in later life. I enjoyed our banter as much as anything else during rehearsals!

[53] I was later to collaborate twice more with Don Lusher in Big Band recordings in Abbey Road Studios. Firstly 'The Big Band Sound' with The Plymouth Band, and, two years later, 'Wind Machine' with the Portsmouth Band. In between these two albums I invited Don to become Professor of Trombone at the RMSM in Portsmouth when I became Director of Music Training. Don stayed with us for 10 years or so in this role.

The arrangement and recording are as popular today as ever before, and it is a constant reminder to me that, with composition, you never know what is around the corner. Who could have predicted this unexpected journey based on a routine piece of work that was only made because of a band engagement we were tasked to perform in the USA. Once something takes off like this there is nothing much you can do to influence it one way or the other. Down the years it has certainly given me notoriety with listeners and with other musicians who I have worked with. For instance, one evening when in the audience at The Royal Albert Hall, the newsreader and author John Suchet (Hercule Poirot's brother!) was in the next box and had heard I was at hand. He asked to meet me because of his admiration for 'The Ashokan' recording and we chatted for some time, making me feel quite the 'star'. This kind of thing happened to me a lot. I sense it was a source of annoyance to some of my fellow Directors of Music. Sorry. It's not my fault.

The recording 'The Ashokan Farewell' (beautifully mastered by Bob Whitney) changed the landscape of military recordings and raised the bar for standards in the future. I had always been trying to make the band sound more like an orchestra with the greater range of colours and a more confident soloistic style, and for the first time we had achieved this. I think we all knew at the time that we were onto something special as a group and we had collectively reinforced so many good musical habits that we could take on ever more challenging music and achieve professional standards with the minimum of rehearsal. Such was the positive atmosphere running through the whole band.

SUMMER 1996
The Band of Her Majesty's Royal Marines, Plymouth

The Plymouth Band of the mid 1990s
The most outstanding musical group I was to lead during my Royal Marines career.
The perfect mix of talent in all ages. Anything was possible!

149

CHAPTER 39

The Big Band Sound
The Band of HM Royal Marines Plymouth
Director of Music: Captain John Perkins LRAM ARCM LGSM RM
Featuring: Don Lusher & Emer McParland
Producer/Editor: Bob Whitney. Engineers: David Flower, Guy Maffey
Recorded at Abbey Road Studio 2, London - 6th & 7th May 1996

Cat. No: CLCD10796

The idea of recording an album of Big Band[54] had been floated many times since the formation of the RM Band Service. At one time there was a more permanent group of RM players gathered together for key events under the title of 'The Oceanairres', the equivalent of the RAF 'Squadronairres'. Many of the players down the years have favoured the 'Big Band' format and we have had countless good Big Band players and jazzers amongst our number. However, there is a big difference between playing this music 'live' and recording it where the level of expertise and accuracy is subject to the forensic test of repeat listening in the cold light of day. In my opinion this project could only work if you were lucky enough to have five good saxophone players in the same band, at least two of whom were outstanding soloists. Piano, bass and drums were generally less of a problem, as was the brass section where the larger bands could generally put a strong team together, although, of course, the stronger the better.

By the time we started on this project we had grown as a super confident band who relished a challenge. We also had a unique band of excellent players in all departments, including, for the first time in my career, five saxophone players who were led by the incomparable Martin Dale, who was by this time also The Bandmaster of the Plymouth Band. Martin and myself went back to the days of Lt Col Paul Neville and the RMSM Staff Band at Deal where, as violinists, we both enjoyed the demands of the orchestral seasons of concerts. At that time Martin was a more than useful violinist and I was Leader of the Orchestra. All these years later Martin had built a strong reputation (which continues to grow to this day) as a terrific Jazz saxophone soloist who had his own instantly recognisable style. He was also a forthright, no-nonsense character who insisted on high standards. We got on very well and made a formidable leadership team, as our priority was always the music.

---

[54] Big Band as in Glenn Miller style music and instrumentation.

We spent a few weeks refining the programme of music to be recorded, sorting out dates, sponsorship and funding to record the album at Abbey Road Studio 2, which had become our favoured inspirational studio. We all realised that we were pioneers in being the first to record a Big Band album so the level of commitment was high. We rehearsed in great detail, both in sectional rehearsals where Martin galvanised the Sax section into ever-greater accuracy and flair, and I the brass in the same fashion. When we came together as a band we could start reinforcing the good habits and tightening up the ensemble sound to make us sound as if we had been playing this music together for years.

Because the project was so special to me I wanted to get a 'headline' Big Band 'star' name to feature on the recording as a soloist, so I asked the renowned trombone legend Don Lusher to join us. Don was a great favourite of Frank Sinatra, Ted Heath and many others. Don couldn't be happier as he had spent his National Service time in The Royal Artillery Band, an experience he thoroughly enjoyed, and had a lasting respect for Military bands, particularly The Royal Marines. I also asked the singer Emma McParland whom I had worked with in Big Band concerts during my time with the Commandos Band. Other solos on the album were covered by the band members where I was spoilt for choice. So we had a plan. Great music, terrific line-up in the band, exceptional soloists, first class studio, producer and engineers and a group of players rehearsed and champing at the bit!

Not only was our time in the studio fun, the results were outstanding and everyone played their socks off! 'The Big Band Sound' remains a landmark recording for the Royal Marines and a superb memory for me and, I hope, others in the band.

75th Anniversary of Abbey Road Studios

As a postscript to the Big Band recording, some months later I had a call from Abbey Road Studios asking whether I could provide a Glen Miller type Big Band to be the studio band for a BBC TV film celebrating the 75th Anniversary of Abbey Road. Being a 'no-brainer' I jumped at the opportunity and we duly became the studio band in the style and uniform of the Glenn Miller band who had recorded there during WW2. During the process of organising this engagement I asked Abbey Road management why they had approached me and The Plymouth Royal Marines Band and not a specialist Big Band. They informed me that they had first approached the Don Lusher Big Band and Don Lusher had recommended my band as the best and most able band he knew of at that time. High praise indeed!

CHAPTER 40

Divisions (in audience)

Down the years I had gained a reputation for avoiding parade work, a well-deserved reputation I concede, but during my time at HMS Raleigh the other officers, and eventually the Captain, got wind of this. One Friday Cay and I were attending a lunch given by the Captain (with whom I got along very well) in Trevol House, the official residence of the Captain of HMS Raleigh. During the very convivial lunch The Captain informed me that he had noticed that I had not been on Friday afternoon Divisions (Parade) for some time, and that he "Would very much like to see me out there this afternoon." Not wishing to defy The Captain, I assured him that I would be out there for Divisions in the afternoon.

Me and Drum Major Harry Roberts on Parade - I told you!

My slight dilemma was that if I appeared with the Band as the conductor (which was clearly what he meant me to do) I would be liable to 'gotcha' comments from the other officers and the band, but I couldn't be seen to defy the Captain. I decided to take a risk, so I went home and changed into full 'Blue' Uniform and Cay and I went back into HMS Raleigh and sat in the chairs immediately alongside the saluting Dais on which the Captain would stand. It was becoming clear to others on the Staff what we were up to.

On The Captain's arrival at the saluting Dais he glanced down at me and mouthed what I took to be 'You Bas…d' and then he carried on with his duties. The subject was never mentioned again, except by some members of the band in the know, who thought my bare-faced cheek was admirable! I continued to enjoy a terrific relationship with the Captain who clearly enjoyed the moment, but couldn't say so in as many words!

The Dream of Gerontius

Without doubt one of the musical highlights (and there were many) were the two performances of Elgar's 'The Dream of Gerontius'[55] given on consecutive nights in St Andrew's Church Plymouth and the Quarterdeck of The Britannia Naval College (BRNC) Dartmouth. The

---

[55] ***The Dream of Gerontius***, Op. 38, is a work for voices and orchestra in two parts composed by Edward Elgar in 1900, to text from the poem by John Henry Newman.

orchestra comprised my players from The Plymouth Band combined with the orchestral players from the BRNC Band. The choir was The Plymouth Philharmonic Choir and the soloists were senior students from the Royal Academy of Music London. Not since the 1970s days of Lt Col Paul Neville and the RMSM orchestra at Deal was this masterpiece attempted by a Royal Marines band. I had led the orchestra for Paul at that time and 'The Dream', Verdi's 'Requiem', Brahms' 'German Requiem' all left a lasting impression on me, but I had long since given up hope of being able to reenact these pieces, especially outside of the School of Music where extra players and rehearsal time were plentiful. However, I now had the finest concert military band I had been part of with many musicians with a similar mindset and ambition as me. Plus, as Director of Music of The Plymouth Band, I could access players from The BRNC which technically came under my command and gave me the extra string players.

The Dream of Gerontius - *Elgar*
Two performances given in St Andrew's Church Plymouth and
Britannia Royal Naval College Dartmouth.

The project was very ambitious both musically and logistically but I was determined to drive it through regardless of the pockets of opposition who could only see the problems. I was aware that The Plymouth Philharmonic Choir was of a good standard and regularly performed large choral works, so I approached their conductor who thought my idea a good one especially as he did not have to pay for the orchestra! After some discussion about conducting, we decided the only workable solution was for me to conduct both performances and for him to conduct the choir rehearsals - result. Having attended The Royal Academy of Music twice as both violinist and conductor I was very aware of the high standard of operatic singing that was always available. I was also aware that the Academy was constantly looking for performance opportunities for its senior students to perform these great works as part of their preparations for the professional world. Having spoken to the Head of Vocal Studies we settled on Henry Moss (Tenor), Nicholas Gedge (Baritone) and Helen Skodge (I think this was the surname of the Mezzo Soprano) as our soloists on the understanding that we would transport them to the West Country, feed and water them, and return them unharmed the following week!

This was a time for taking a few risks, so I put (young) Musician Ashley Williams[56] in as Leader of the orchestra and (young) Musician Mark Phillips[57] as principal cello. They both did an exceptional job. I asked an old friend WO2 Bandmaster Paul Weston (later to become Director of Music of the Plymouth Band as Major) to come from Deal to lead the violas. I also had WO2 Bandmaster Martin Dale fit into the centre of the 1st violins and add his ability and confidence to the team. There were plenty of other good string players who were up for the challenge from both my band and BRNC, albeit almost nobody had played the 'Dream' before. We rehearsed in sections in the mornings for several days getting together in the afternoon for full orchestra sessions, and, inch-by-inch, we prepared for the choir rehearsals. At the same time my admin team was preparing a plan for all the other transport, accommodation, catering, staging, lighting and other logistics involved in the two venues we were to perform. I am not saying it was an easy project, and I am not saying everyone enjoyed the music as much as I did, but I am saying this was exactly what we should have been doing to develop younger members of the band and show just what The Royal Marines Band Service could achieve. The performances in Plymouth and Dartmouth were triumphs and I loved every minute of it, as did the choirs, the soloists and the vast majority of the orchestra. This was one of the most satisfying projects of my service career. Loved it!

'Listen to The Band' broadcast

The reputation of the Plymouth Band had spread around the military music world, mostly because of the recordings we had made, but also because of the superb concerts we played around the country on a regular basis. As a result we were approached by the BBC to record an edition of the BBC programme 'Listen To The Band'. We recorded this programme for the BBC

---

[56] Ashley was a gifted all-round musician who was a joy to have in the band. He went on to become a highly respected Warrant Officer Bandmaster and special human being. I always expected him to become a Director of Music.

[57] Mark was another superb young prospect on both Euphonium and especially cello. A more enthusiastic and committed member of the Band Service it would be hard to find. Mark has served in recent years as The Band Secretary of The Plymouth Band.

in Plymouth Guildhall over two sessions on the same day. Our programme of music included the cornet solo 'Napoli' a classic showpiece of the repertoire. The incomparable Ivan Hutchinson played 'Napoli' superbly, as did Barry Hill with the oboe solo 'Gabriel's Oboe' which I had arranged for Barry to play on 'The Ashokan Farewell' album. We also included the three movements of 'Theatre Music' by Philip Sparke, a composer I much enjoyed. I listened again to this recording recently and was struck by the quality of the playing by the band. The confidence and flair for which we had very quickly become known was impressive. The BBC presenter Frank Renton (an old friend, excellent musician and former Principal Director of Music of the Corps of Army Music) called me to say how impressed he was with our band and that he believed we were probably the finest military band in the country at that time. Rare praise for the Royal Marines from such a central figure in Army music!

Moving on all too soon

I left the Plymouth Band with much regret having petitioned my bosses to stay and finish my remaining few years with the band before retiring. My request was refused so, in a little less than 20 months, I was on the move again to take Command of the newly located Royal Marines School of Music at Portsmouth. I left a 'world-class' band full of 'world-class' people feeling pretty angry at being moved just prior to the opening of the new bandroom, which was my 'baby', and returning to the Headquarters Band Service, which was my nemesis! Arghhhh!

John conducting The Plymouth Big Band for the documentary
of the 75th Anniversary of Abbey Road Studios

CHAPTER 41

Portsmouth - Director of Music Training (DOMT)

I arrived in Portsmouth to a fairly confusing scene of the RMSM having been 'crowbarred' into the old Naval Detention Quarters in The Naval Dockyard, with scant facilities. The Band Service Headquarters was setting itself up in the middle of the Portsmouth/Royal Yacht Band accommodation together with the new elements of Instrument Repair and the Central Music Library.

The newly relocated Music School in the old Detention Quarters in Portsmouth Dockyard was an ugly and depressing place (after all it was a prison!), and was the subject of great mirth by all and sundry especially some senior officers who saw it as a novel use of what were unusable historic buildings - *e.g.* a problem solved. I never shared this collective humour and so I went to Portsmouth, somewhat kicking and screaming. This also meant another disruption for the family who now had to move again after only 20 months, as there was no prospect of me returning to Plymouth.

Shortly after I arrived in Portsmouth a very senior RM Officer, who shall remain nameless, a pompous man who found the whole situation of the RMSM very amusing, came by my office with his wife to discuss a future event for which the trainees were providing the music. He thought it was hilarious that we were occupying prison cells to train musicians and was so proud he had saved money by closing the barracks at Deal and relocating the RMSM to the Detention Quarters at virtually zero cost. He exuded all the worst traits of a Public School twit, a man who almost fell over his own sense of entitlement. He was easy to dislike! I listened to him - as I had to - and at a certain point he asked, "And what are you doing next?" I replied, "I'm going home to watch Eastenders to keep in touch with the real world!" I never watched Eastenders or any soap, and it wasn't the best line, but I wanted to say something to take the edge off his pomposity. He left very shortly afterwards, and my self-destruct button was back in action!

Within the new setup in Portsmouth there were power struggles at all levels and I found myself in some type of job-sharing arrangement with a General List Officer (non-musician) on The Headquarters Band Service (HQBS) staff, which was a frequent source of conflict. Coincidentally we were old friends from the Deal Bombing time, but we were both determined characters who resented the interference of the other. The difficulties remained for the whole of my time in this job, although things are very different today I am pleased to say. My Chief Instructor WO1 Bandmaster Bob Metcalf, a contemporary of mine and good friend, was also the Corps Bandmaster working in the Band Service Headquarters, causing another conflict of priorities (although Bob was terrific as far as I was concerned).

The worst example of The HQBS coming up with the wrong answer was early on in my tenure when I met a Naval Lieutenant Commander in the Wardroom Mess whom I had been friendly with in Plymouth. We chatted about our respective new jobs and I explained to him the conditions of our new School of Music and the lack of equipment, particularly computers and music software etc. Coincidentally he held the budget for computers on behalf of the Portsmouth Command and had a large underspend for that current financial year. He asked what I needed and how much it would cost. I said we would need lots of Apple Mac computers as our need would be for graphics/sound technology-based activities, and the cost would be around £250K, a figure I plucked out of the air! He said if I put my justification for funding in a paper, explaining the special Apple Mac requirement of the Band Service, he would try to back the case, but it had to be done right away to use the underspend for that financial year. As it happened I already had a good case stored on my (personal) computer from something similar I had done whilst SO(M) some years earlier, so I revamped my earlier work and got it across to him within a couple of days.

Almost by return I had an email saying my request was approved to a limit of £220K and I now needed to be more specific with computer models and software so purchase contracts could be placed. Result!

I took my good news over to The HQBS expecting an enthusiastic response and explaining the urgency of the time constraint, less we lose the underspend. Sadly they wanted to consider this proposal further and convened a meeting amongst themselves the following week. From this meeting (I was not present) their decision was that they wanted to base this procurement on 'Acorn' computers as Acorn had the 'Sibelius' music software embedded in the operating system!! I couldn't believe it as we were discarding a top-end Apple system for 'Acorn' which at the time was thought to be close to going out of business - which it did shortly afterwards. Also it was widely reported that 'Sibelius' software was soon to be launched on the Apple platform - which it was. I tried as best I could to persuade HQBS of their folly but they were adamant. So with reluctance I passed this new information back to my Lt Cdr colleague who said he could not support this change to Acorn, so the funding was withdrawn and we ended up with nothing. It took several more years to begin the procurement of Apple computers, long after Acorn was forgotten about and long after I had left the Band Service!

Apart from the shortage of facilities across the board, other important issues were sitting on my desk, the two most important being a proposed degree accreditation proposal from the University of Portsmouth and the recently established Armed Forces Bursary Scheme. This bursary scheme was an ill-thought-out tri-service cost-cutting exercise that had serious consequences and took another year or more to eventually scrap.

CHAPTER 42

The Armed Forces Bursary Scheme

T he thinking behind this scheme was that music, being a civilian subject, could be taught in a large number of civilian institutions at a much lower cost and, when graduated, the student could come and join a military band, thus preventing the need to run military music schools. Each Bursary student having shown an interest in joining a military band would be paid a bursary of £500 per term while they were studying and still part of the scheme. There was no legal compulsion to join The Royal Marines/Army/RAF when students graduated. What?

The first tri-service meeting I attended in Whitehall on the subject was shortly after my arrival in Portsmouth. My predecessor had given me the impression that, albeit as yet unproven, he was open to this Bursary Scheme and he saw the scheme as a potential alternative to having to run a school of music - although to be fair, it was early days and he did have reservations. The meetings were chaired by an Army Brigadier who was not a musician and had no background of working with bands much less the music schools. I remember an upbeat atmosphere in the room as we all introduced ourselves and listened to updates from various representatives from the three services. Almost all reports given were positive. My instincts were crying out 'No', this is littered with unanswered questions.

I had made a few notes before attending the meeting, such as:

1. What do we do about assessing our bursary students throughout their training?
2. What do we do about training these students in secondary instruments to meet the unique requirements of the Naval Service?
3. What do we do about Buglers Training (1-year 8 month course) that has no civilian equivalent?
4. What do we do about higher training for promotion and advancement to SNCO, Warrant Officer and Commissioned Officer?
5. What do we do about parade training to become proficient in marching bands?

The biggest problem was not visible at this time. Some months later John Hillier (our man in the RM Headquarters) discovered that all funding for a RM music school had been deleted from the long-term costings for the Royal Marines based on the early indications that this scheme would work!

When it came to my turn to report on behalf of the RMs I went through my list sensing the early 'bonhomie' dissipate as I was talking. I finally made the point that, as a new member of this working group, I may be worrying unnecessarily as these issues may have been covered in earlier meetings. Of course I knew they hadn't as I had read the minutes.

The Brigadier responded that all these concerns were easily remedied. I pressed him on the assessment of students saying that it was fundamental to any meaningful reporting in this forum that we assess the bursary students ourselves on a regular basis to track their progress. Until this point it was assumed that the university or college would carry out this function. Reluctantly, or maybe to shut me up, The Brigadier conceded the point and it was agreed we could make our own assessments to monitor progress. Other points I raised were left unanswered, but they would form the basis of future meetings.

Over the next few months I arranged to get all the bursary students into Portsmouth to give them an acquaint on The Royal Marines Band Service and allow us an opportunity to hear them play. Quite by chance this coincided with a BBC South TV feature on the new School that was being filmed during the same few days. We had agreed that the TV company should have unfettered access to what we were doing in our new music school, its site in the old detention quarters having generated considerable interest. As part of this access I did a piece to camera about the bursary scheme, which was followed by the BBC filming a few of the students playing their chosen pieces. Oh dear!

There were two or three proficient players among the bursary students, but sadly most were poor and, when it came to the second instrument they were learning from scratch in order to comply with the RN requirement, some were totally hopeless - complete beginners. Clearly they had not been taking this part of their studies seriously. This was when 'sod's law' kicked in, and one of the most inept students came into the room at the very time the TV crew were setup and ready to film. Of course I wasn't to know this, as I had not heard any of them before this point in time. The student in question, a female studying in a University not known for its music degree, came in carrying a saxophone and violin. I asked her a few questions to try to put her at her ease and then invited her to play us something on both instruments. She started on the saxophone which was her first study instrument. It was not good and I was starting to get a little hot under the collar as the TV crew was filming the whole process. A little earlier I had been explaining to camera that the Royal Marines School of Music was one of the finest music institutions in the country and without doubt one of the premier military music schools in the world!

I intervened with the saxophone presentation and invited the young lady to play us a little on her violin. Wrong! Although she had been studying the violin for almost four terms she had no idea how to hold the instrument properly and could barely play the most simple scales or pieces. Very embarrassing. I stopped her quickly and thanked her for coming in to see us etc….

And that was it. The film crew packed their kit away and moved on to their next location which had all been pre-arranged. And so it was that when the programme was broadcast some days later, right on cue, there she was playing her saxophone and violin for the whole world to witness! If I needed evidence that this bursary scheme was a complete sham there it was, in spades. From that moment I devoted much time and energy to discrediting the scheme to the Brigadier and others on the steering group. It was not working as it was setup to do and left so many unanswered questions about other training issues I had previously raised. I think the bursary scheme ran for two years and was eventually discontinued. From this experimental scheme three students did join us and they were all very good prospects. Notwithstanding their civilian BMus degree, they still needed to complete the whole of our internal instrumental course of 2 years 8 months. Two of the three went on to have illustrious careers. Ross Hunt (recently retired) became a highly successful WO1 Bandmaster and Tom Crane became a commissioned officer and is currently serving as a Captain Director of Music.

This whole process had taught me some important lessons about the wide variety of standards in music degree institutions around the country, and I became ever more persuaded that the proposal to achieve degree accreditation for Royal Marines music training through The University of Portsmouth should be pursued if at all possible - and it was possible.

CHAPTER 43

The Degree Accreditation Programme

Over the course of my career I had seen major changes in attitudes to academic study. In the late 1960s my violin teacher told me in clear terms not to make too much of any academic study when auditioning for orchestras as such study was seen as a distraction from the priority of instrumental practice. Time spent on academic study was time not spent on practicing! Conservatories, where performance excellence was the aim, were the mainstream and music degree study was the preserve of a few universities where the performance skills were secondary to academic work. Over the years, changes in Higher education would see a major shift in this policy and by the 1990s all music study in Conservatories and universities was accredited for degrees. Many more universities were offering music degrees and standards varied enormously from one place to another, as I was discovering with The Armed Forces Bursary Scheme.

The music degree was suddenly vital for employment opportunities in education and the degree had become the 'guarantee' of a comprehensive training. Yet my experience of visiting students in a wide variety of music institutions around the country, monitoring the bursary scheme was showing me that this was far from any type of guarantee. The majority of students I came into contact with knew next to nothing about the history of Western Art music, harmony, composition and orchestration, even the basic elements of music. In most cases their practical performance skills were also well short of the basic requirement to be in a Royal Marines band. I must say that this was a confusing picture for me, as up to this point I had no idea the world around us had changed so much. We were being left behind with qualifications and our people were at a disadvantage when competing with civilians who had a music degree, however worthless!

The Band Service had always had its own qualifications from instrumental New Entry training through to Director of Music. The standards were high and the training was comprehensive. Higher Training courses were in-depth, intensive and relevant to the work of a professional musician. Bandmaster and Director of Music courses were monitored by The Royal Academy of Music London which was one of the flagship music institutions in the world. We had been getting it right for years, yet our qualifications were not understood in the civilian world. Times were changing and we needed to offer our own people and new trainees qualifications they could use in their futures. Our training across the board was tougher than most all civilian institutions yet it was not accredited for degrees. So it was with a sense of destiny that I got together with Dr William McVicker (BA, PhD, LRAM, ARCO, Hon ARAM, Hon FIMIT) the Director of Music of The University of Portsmouth, to discuss the possibility of the University of Portsmouth accrediting our training for civilian recognised qualifications.

William and I hit it off straight away. We had our own agendas, mine to right the wrongs outlined above, William's to raise the profile of music within the University which currently only offered music as an extracurricular activity. It was an ambitious project that took 15 months to complete and required 220,000 words of documentation before we achieved accreditation at both Bachelors (BMus) and Masters (MMus) levels. Strangely enough the greatest obstacles came from within the Band Service itself, from some of the Directors of Music and NCOs who saw the whole exercise as an 'unnecessary distraction'. During the process we toured all the bands and gave presentations on our proposals inviting comments and criticisms etc. Although the initial response was disappointing, the tide of opinion began to change and it was soon considered to be the most positive improvement to recruiting and retention The Band Service had achieved. Many of the early critics benefited from the scheme and qualified themselves before moving into civilian life - funny old thing!

As part of the new relationship with the University of Portsmouth we combined for weekly orchestral and band rehearsals which helped both parties perform as larger groups and in turn opened up new repertoire. The University is sited almost alongside HMS Nelson where the RMSM was now based, so it was a short walk for everyone to get together. We gave joint concerts in Portsmouth and I felt that both parties were benefiting from the collaboration.

The process of documenting the Royal Marines courses into degree credits via assessments proved more problematic and was initially viewed with some suspicion within the RMSM. The Academic Professor Liz Le Grove (who I liked a great deal, and was an excellent appointment for The RMSM) and the newly appointed piano professor Rob Douglas (responsible for the academic training of students on the initial 2 years 8 months instrumental course) were as keen as us to get this right. Rob and Liz became the key players in the degree process which they have continued to develop down the years. They are both still in post 25 years later and have provided great expertise and continuity for the School.

There were plenty of sceptics in The Band Service and some who felt it was all happening with undue haste, but I knew, having been involved with large-scale projects before, that momentum was essential. Any delay would most likely lead to the whole project being kicked into the long grass. It seemed obvious that we would have just one shot at getting this done before I was moved on to my last job and I saw nobody coming up behind eager to take this on. So, in my judgement, it was time to seize the moment and get this past the finish line. Once achieved there would be many years to fine tune the degree, but we had to get our training accredited whilst we had the goodwill, momentum and funding. As the months unfolded, trust and cooperation between all parties prevailed and, after much intense detailed work, we did achieve degree accreditation at the first attempt. Everyone had realised that the prize was too great to let this slip through our fingers.

Dr William McVicker, already a successful recording artist, author and teacher, resigned from the University of Portsmouth in late 1998 to pursue his performance and writing career. His departure left The University without the musical expertise to support The RMSM degree programme. Not surprisingly, in 2013 (some 15 years later), the RMSM signed a deal with The University of Plymouth to replace Portsmouth, since when the relationship with Plymouth has continued to flourish.

William currently teaches Organology at the Royal Academy of Music. He is Organ Curator for the Royal Festival Hall at the Southbank Centre and is a firm favourite with Classic FM where he is heard regularly as an organist.

Together, I think we achieved something remarkable and I look back on this achievement with a sense of pride. Whatever relationships are being enjoyed now by the RMSM and University of Plymouth are based on the genuine hard work we put in to getting this ambitious project up and running. I look back at this time as a pioneering achievement for the Band Service that transformed recruiting, retention and retirement prospects for the next generation of Royal Marines musicians.

Odds and Ends

During the first year the RMSM was in the former Detention Quarters it was not rare for unexpected visitors to pop in to see for themselves just how the new setup was working out for music training. One afternoon WO2 Bandmaster Dave Wilson (who worked in the office next to mine) received a telephone call 'tipping us the wink' that HRH Prince Philip had been spotted walking unescorted towards the RMSM. Dave wanted no part of the reception committee, so I put my cap on and ventured out to intercept HRH. Prince Philip was Captain General of the Royal Marines at the time, so he wanted to see the new music school for himself. I met HRH just inside the gate and showed him around the practice rooms (previously locked cells) and the small estate of basic buildings that surrounded the prison block. I was pleased the Captain General arrived unannounced because he got the unvarnished tour without all the formalities that usually accompany Royal visits.

He took in everything, including the music trainees going about their normal duties, and he appeared genuinely interested in what he saw. We agreed that there was much work to be done. He thanked me and was gone, walking back into HMS Nelson by himself. I'd forgotten about this cameo Royal visit until Dave Wilson reminded recently. Unannounced visits seem so much more productive - in my opinion.

CHAPTER 44

Buglers Training

If I were to identify one section of the Band Service above all others that made the most progress throughout my career I would have to say the Buglers Branch. This had a major boost in the 1990s, more especially during my time as DOM(T) 1996-98, when under the leadership of Corps Bugle Major Bob Platts a new vision for the branch emerged from Bob and his team. Bob was a musical man who was not satisfied with the status quo, and saw the answer to achieving real progress very much based in training. Bob fought for and achieved professors lessons on both bugle and drum for all new entry buglers as well as producing a body of written work towards civilian accreditation. When one sees the finished product of buglers training in the many high-profile engagements undertaken throughout the year it is a wonderful testament to Bob and those whose careers he touched such as A J Piner. No doubt Bob Platts will be remembered for the important part he played. I hope so.

The Buglers Branch also provided the vast majority of Drum Majors from its number and it was my privilege to serve with some of the best, starting in Portsmouth with Colin Bowden, John Porter and Brian Peaver (the perfect Royal Yacht DM). All very different characters, but equally effective with their own individual skills and personalities. From those I served with as a DOM, the Drum Majors who seemed on the same page as me were Keith Pullen, Phil Hayward, Harry Roberts, Steve Muddiman, Andy Bridges, James 'Wiggy' Whitwham and Lee Hodges. Of course there were many more, but our paths never (or only briefly) crossed or my memory has failed me!

It was enjoyable to attend the 2019 RMSM Open Day in Portsmouth and see the buglers fully integrated in the performances including singing in the choir! Not something seen in earlier times, that's for sure. I was always a champion of the Buglers Branch. I was convinced that The Buglers Branch gave the Royal Marines something unique that could not be replicated in The Army or RAF Music Services. This is still the case.

Other Highlights from this time

Overall, I greatly enjoyed my time as Director of Music (Training). I enjoyed the recruitment process of seeing young boys and girls present themselves for audition and progress into our numbers to undergo the 2 years 8 months basic training course, witnessing their remarkable progress in our unique system of full-time training. Under the supervision of specialist instrumental professors, from whom they received two one-to-one lessons each week on each instrument, and the constant advice and tutorship of uniformed instructors, progress was rapid. The minimum contact time each week between staff and students was 40 hours on top of which were group activities such as band and orchestral rehearsals that took place in the evenings. The training was intensive and competitive and saw remarkable success stories, with the most talented achieving stunning results. I even recruited my old friend Alan Upton's son Mark as a solo cornet player in 1995, since when Mark has blossomed into one of the finest Trumpet players in the country. It was rewarding being responsible for this whole area.

The Higher Training Department was also a major part of my domain, where the two main courses were the eight weeks M1s Course for advancement to SNCO, and the 1-year Bandmasters' Course which was a truly valuable experience for anyone. The main subjects were conducting and orchestration/composition. Other key areas were The History of Western Music, aural training, general musical knowledge (Viva Voce) and the wider aspects of musical leadership. This course was and is a model of quality in musical education the like of which cannot be found anywhere else in the UK (that I am aware of).

I also enjoyed the concert opportunities that arose during my time at the School. The piano professor Rob Douglas had quickly become a friend and we have shared a number of very enjoyable performances down the years, the highlight of which was a performance of the Grieg Piano Concerto we gave at one of the winter series of orchestral concerts in Portsmouth. I remember this performance clearly, as I do all the chamber music concerts we gave together when I had retired from the Royal Marines. Another memorable concert I conducted with the joint orchestras of the RMSM and The University of Portsmouth included a complete performance of Symphony No 3 by Saint-Saëns (The Organ Symphony). It was somewhat of a triumph to achieve such a creditable performance of this complicated orchestral work with the Training orchestra.

Back to the Violin

During the late 1990s, my recording (and musical arrangement) of 'The Ashokan Farewell' (recorded in Abbey Road Studios in 1995) was gaining some traction in radio stations and was increasingly broadcast on Classic FM. Because of this I was asked to play the piece in the Mountbatten Festival of Music in February 1998 in London's Royal Albert Hall. There were three consecutive nightly performances and my performance was received with huge enthusiasm. Sir Paul Condon's decision to include our recording in his Desert Island Discs was a stroke of luck/fate allowed the recording to be heard to a much wider Radio 2 audience, and the rest, as they say, is history.

Such was the enthusiasm for my 'Ashokan' performance that the following year (1999) I was asked to play 'Schindler's List' for the three nights of MFM. By this time I was Director of Music Portsmouth, so I was also conducting in the concerts. It is not easy (or wise) to change in the same concert from conducting, which requires waving your arms around, to playing the violin, especially for such a delicate piece as John Williams' 'Schindler's List'. This was a less comfortable experience than the previous year as I was positioned about 20 feet away (and in front) from the accompanying band (creating a slight time delay) and had a conductor who was following the music, basically behind the beat. Add to this playing in Mess Dress ('made to measure' for me 15 years earlier!) and I was quite relieved when the concerts were over. The next time I was to play a solo in London's Royal Albert Hall was as a civilian in 2001 with The Royal Philharmonic Orchestra in a live broadcast for Classic FM. I made a point of standing in the traditional place with orchestra and wore clothes that fitted me!

I would have happily carried on as Director of Music Training for the remaining 20 months of my service before retirement…………….. but no! Towards the end of my time as DOM(T) I was summoned to the Officers Promotion Board to be told formally that it had been decided that I was not going to be promoted to PDM[58]. Although highly recommended, the reason given was that the current PDM was so close to me in age that it made more sense to give him a two-year extension and then select a younger man, rather than give me a three-year extension to make the promotion worthwhile. Given that I already knew this, the whole process was a little unnecessary. I was not disappointed as I had never expected a different outcome. Given the circumstances, I would have made the same decision.

With less than two years left to serve I was reappointed as The Director of Music of The Band of HM Royal Marines Portsmouth (Royal Band) - the band where it all began for me back in 1968!

---

[58] I wasn't even aware I was under consideration!

CHAPTER 45

The Portsmouth Band (Royal Band)

The appointment as DOM of the Portsmouth Band (Royal Band) was my 4th appointment in 6 years - one too many in my opinion. No sooner had I become established at CTCRM, Plymouth and the RMSM and I was moved - again. I have my theory why this was the case, but I shall keep that to myself. However, I was pleased to be back with a band if only for 20 months, especially the band where life was so good to me when I started out in the Band Service. I even teamed up again with my old friend and Bandmaster of the Commandos Band Clive Close, who was now the WO1 Bandmaster of the Portsmouth Band.

They say timing is everything, and here was a case in point. I would have loved to have had the opportunity to serve once again in HMY Britannia, especially as the Director of Music - a perfect symmetry for a 35-year career. Sadly this was not to be as Britannia was withdrawn from service the year before I arrived on the scene. Such was the pent-up frustration of an incoming Labour government in 1997 who had had Britannia firmly in their crosshairs for many years. The loss of HMY Britannia had a profound effect on those who served in her over the years since 1954. This very much included the RM Band members, many of whom had served for more than a decade in the Yacht Band. Their reluctance to take down their distinctive 'Royal Yacht' shoulder flashes was easily understood by me as an ex-Yachty myself, but when I arrived in the band, some nine months after Britannia had been decommissioned, there were still two separate parts to the Portsmouth Band. On the one hand the original members of the Portsmouth Band who had served prior to the amalgamation of the Deal Staff Band within the Portsmouth setup in 1996, and those members of the Staff Band who had moved to Portsmouth on the closure of Deal.

The 'them and us' atmosphere was plain to see through the shoulder flashes, and the feeling of being slightly unwelcome newcomers was felt by a sizeable number of colleagues from Deal. It was not a healthy situation to allow to continue, so I made this a priority by insisting that all Yacht Flashes were taken down immediately and those few die-hards who were clinging to the past had the option to leave the band. Nobody left! I am always amazed to see how quickly people accept a refreshed situation as long as it is made clear from the start, with no room for negotiation. Within a few short weeks we were all pulling in the same direction and planning new concerts and recordings as well as all the routine band engagements in the Portsmouth Command. A few months later Queen Elizabeth bestowed the honour of 'Royal Band' on the Portsmouth Band since when the whole band wears the shoulder flash 'Royal Band'.

The Band Service numbered some 430 all ranks (at that time) and was small enough to know everyone to a greater or lesser degree. The programme of events leading into the Christmas period had been in place for many years, starting with Christmas concerts in late November! There was a run of 16 concerts in 18 days in early December ranging from 5 days in the Chichester Theatre to mini tours of the Midlands and a series of concerts along the South Coast. A gruelling schedule, but the very stuff of creating a corporate spirit and getting used to me as a conductor. Once the early suspicions of me had passed we got along very well and, again, I had an abundance of talent in the band which started my imagination racing as to potential future recordings.

Songs of the Sea

The Band of HM Royal Marines Portsmouth (Royal Band)
Director of Music: Major John Perkins MMus ARAM ARCM LGSM RM
The Royal Marines School of Music Choir (Chorus Master Emer McParland)
Soloist: William Shimell (Baritone)
Producer: Bob Whitney, Engineers: Tony Faulkner. Editor: Bob Whitney
Recorded at Abbey Road Studio 1, London - 20th and 21st January 1999

Although my time with the Portsmouth Band was inevitably short with a compulsory retirement age of 50 years only 20 months away, I was nevertheless keen to make the most of the time and recordings were never far from my mind. This was partly because I loved the whole recording process and partly because I knew, for sure, that making new recordings, as long as they were well prepared and recorded, would inevitably raise the musical standard of the band. My association with the RNLI and Brian Williams and his West Country Marketing Group (*see Appendix 2*) went back to my time with the Commandos Band when we recorded the first in the RNLI series, 'Marches of the Sea', which was made to record Musician Trevor Brown's new march 'The

Cat. No: CLCD10999

Lifeboatmen'. I first met Brian during my tour as Director of Music of FOPs Band in the mid 1980s when Brian was a strong supporter of the band at concerts and a great encouragement to me personally. Brian, an ex-Royal Marines Officer, lived in his retirement in Kingsand, Cornwall, a short drive from HMS Raleigh where the band was based. Another of his interests was the Rame Peninsula Male Voice Choir which I too became involved with as I invited them to join me and the band in concert in the Roebuck Theatre, HMS Raleigh. In preparation for this concert I attended a couple of choir rehearsals so we could get to know each other. The choir was a decent standard and full of great characters who loved to sing, particularly in the pub after the rehearsal when all the good work done at the rehearsal was forgotten! On one occasion whilst conducting I became aware of a very powerful 'high quality' voice emerging from within the choir, clearly nothing I had heard before. When we stopped for a break I got amongst the choir to identify the voice that turned out to be the son of one of the choir members, who was back in the area on holiday. His name was William Shimell, an operatic 'principal' at Covent Garden Opera and many of the leading opera houses in Europe and the United States. What a voice.

I would go on to invite William to sing with the band on a number of occasions during the 1980s, so when the opportunity came to make a recording of Charles Villiers Standford's 'Songs of the Sea' and 'Songs of the Fleet' a decade later William[59] was the obvious choice as soloist. In truth I had wanted to undertake this complicated project for a long time. The project required a new concert band arrangement of both pieces to be custom made, a world class baritone solo voice, a choir and a full concert band. My old friends Andy Thornhill and Sid Davis made the band arrangements for me with great skill and much hard work on their part. My successor as DOM (Training) in The RMSM Major Chris Davis agreed that I could use the RMSM choir[60] under the direction of Emer McParland and, of course, William Shimell as the soloist. We booked Abbey Road Studios for the recording and Clovelly Recordings Ltd financed and produced the whole project, with some sponsorship from the RNLI. Game on!

This recording was wildly ambitious and very expensive, but what a rewarding experience for us all and terrific music to play and sing. We even hired the Abbey Road house alongside the Studios to stay for the three days of the recording. My old friend Ken Peers joined William and me for the stay to observe our Principal Engineer Tony Faulkner at work. Tony was and is one of London's best and it was interesting that just recently he was recording the Mountbatten Festival of Music in 2020, 21 years after Songs of the Sea. Tony would also engineer another recording later that year with me in Chichester Cathedral with the Band and the Cathedral Choir entitled 'A Christmas Festival'.

---

[59] Who had offered his services free of charge as the project was for the RNLI.

[60] I had previously approached the Royal Academy of Music Choir to act as the choir for this recording which was agreed, but ended up conflicting with an Academy production of an opera when we had to change our dates.

CHAPTER 46

The Cut and Thrust of serving alongside the Headquarters Band Service

The cut and thrust of serving alongside the Headquarters Band Service was the thing I really disliked about the new arrangements in Portsmouth. The amalgamation of the RMSM and Headquarters Band Service in the same geographical space as the Portsmouth Band was a bad idea from the start and caused confusion as to who was in charge of the band. My predecessor David Cole had been told by the Principal Director that he was Director of Music of the band in the normal way - no change. However, because David was away with the Royal Yacht Band in Britannia for much of his time, the remainder of the band was run by the Bandmaster, so the impact on David as DOM was minimal. When I took over the band in 1998 I was told the same arrangements would apply and so I proceeded on that basis. Unfortunately there was no Royal Yacht to take refuge in!

It immediately became obvious that the use of the band was divided three ways between me, The Principal Director of Music and the Director of Music Training. The PDM used the band for events he had brought with him from Deal, all massed bands events and National ceremonies, such as The RBL Festival of Remembrance in The Royal Albert Hall when he would be in command. This was of course his prerogative. The Director of Music Training would be in command of all Higher Training courses which included eight winter season public concerts for trainee Bandmasters to conduct. Each of these public concerts required the whole band and took a minimum of a week to rehearse and perform.

Add all the above together and there were very few opportunities left for me as the Director of the Band to get involved with music. For much of my short time with the band I seemed to be writing reports on everyone and dealing with all the routine matters of being a 'Divisional Officer' for the 80 or so people (technically) under my command. Others seemed to be doing the musical bits of my job. Quite a different role than when I was last in the band during the 70s. Not really what I had in mind!

Although assured otherwise I always thought this would be the case, hence my reluctance to leave my previous job. Although I found the 'job-share' frustrating I knew my days left in the Band Service were numbered so I accepted the situation with good grace and concentrated on the concerts and recordings that presented themselves, in the certain knowledge that I couldn't change this new status quo anyway. It was my view at the time that the PDM should have formally assumed ownership of the Portsmouth Band and nominated a (more junior) Director of Music to be his assistant, much as it had been in Deal since the 1950s. A clear decision and clean break from the past would have done the trick! To try to please everyone was never going to please anyone.

CHAPTER 47

The Pride and Passion (15 Great English Rugby Anthems)
The Band of HM Royal Marines Portsmouth (Royal Band)
Director of Music: Major John Perkins MMus ARAM ARCM LGSM RM
The Honey Male Voice Choir (Choir Master: Sean De Burca)
Producer: Chris Walker
Recorded at Angel Studios, London in May 1999

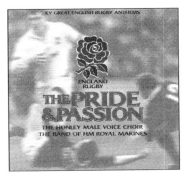

Cat. No: RFU CD1

I can truthfully say that I was pleased with all recordings I made with RM bands throughout my career as Director of Music. I felt that we were always well prepared and rehearsed to 'peak' at the right time. The music was carefully researched and each piece was either an original composition or a high-quality arrangement. I also kept control of who was to be the engineers and producer of each recording, and, of equal importance, the Editing and Mastering of the recordings. Even when Ken Peers and myself started back in 1985 in Plymouth with our 'in house' studio, no stone was unturned in search of the best quality and, back then, we went to Abbey Road Studios to have the recordings Mastered. For the first time in my career I felt as if this recording fell short of the standards I would normally consider acceptable. No fault of the band, who played beautifully as ever, and were well rehearsed going into the sessions.

The idea of this recording was not a bad one as it would be released just prior to the Rugby World Cup, hopefully appealing to the patriotic English rugby fans. The recording was sponsored by First Night Records, who are a company based in the West End of London whose catalogue of recordings was essentially the original cast recordings of the West End musicals. The introduction was written by the former England Captain Bill Beaumont and included 15 titles such as Land of Hope and Glory, I Vow to Thee my Country, Jerusalem, Rule Britannia, Swing Low Sweet Chariot - you get the picture. The excellent Honley Male Voice Choir was to join us as the choir. When it was pitched to me I thought, 'Yes, bring it on'.

However, my obsession with quality was not matched by the record company who were not really on the same page. Firstly the musical arrangements were average at best and poor in some cases. I offered to put this right or get others to do better, but they were committed to what they had already arranged. Further, they had booked The Angel Studios in London which, albeit a good studio, was too small for a large concert band and choir. So the recording was planned to be made in two separate parts, firstly the band backing parts in Angel Studios, then they would take the edited backing tracks to Huddersfield to record the choir over the backing tracks. Why not Abbey Road Studio 1 or Henry Wood Hall? Cost maybe? Worse still, for political reasons, they wanted to use two conductors, me for the backing tracks and the Choir MD for the choir some weeks later. It really does need to have the same conductor for both parts if this is the chosen route in order to synchronise the two parts and disguise the dislocated recording process. Having said all the above, the recording was not dreadful it just wasn't as good as it should have been.

The Portsmouth 'Big Band' with Don Lusher and Emer McParland
Sony Studios London

Given that I had spent so much of my conducting life hugely interested and active in recording, I found this experience very disappointing and frustrating. I hope I never showed my frustration to my band, but I was left feeling this was potentially a good project that ended up short-changed. However, it also vindicated my determination to go my own way with recordings, choosing who I worked with and keeping control of all aspects of the process for the previous fifteen years. Thank goodness I did.

Wind Machine
The Band of HM Royal Marines Portsmouth (Royal Band)
Featuring: Emer McParland & Don Lusher
Director of Music: Major John Perkins MMus ARAM ARCM LGSM RM
Band Leader/Trainer: Band Colour Sergeant George Tate
Producer & Editor: Bob Whitney, Engineers: Mike Ross-Trevor & David Russell
Recorded at Sony Studios, London on 21st & 22nd July 1999

Another significant and enjoyable recording was a Big Band (Glen Miller style/size band) recording entitled 'Wind Machine'. Ever since recording 'The Big Band Sound' with the Plymouth Band in 1996 the interest in Big Band music had flourished and most bands included a section of their concerts as a Big Band feature. In truth, I never believed I would have another band capable of pulling this off, but such was the enthusiasm in the Portsmouth Band for a Big Band recording that it became silly not to go ahead.

Cat. No: CLCD11499

The recording took its title from the Sammy Nestico fast tempo composition called 'Wind Machine'. The remainder of the music was chosen by George Tate and the band, as music they enjoyed playing and which had not previously been previously recorded by a RM band. The CD was recorded at Sony Studios, London on 21st & 22nd July 1999. The result makes for extremely enjoyable listening with both the quality of the playing and the variety of content. It is not until re-listening to recordings years after they were made that you can get a sense as to where the quality level is. This recording really does stand the test of time. I had some very strong players in the band and more than a few who were noted jazz/dance band/big band specialists. Add to this Don Lusher and Emer McParland and it was a potent mix. Looking through the list of the players today, I can see Musician Richard Harvey on 1st Trombone. Richard went on to become a very talented Director of Music. Also Band Sergeant Jason Bircham on Piano. Jason is currently The Principal Director of Music Royal Marines in the rank of Lieutenant Colonel. A happy experience for us all.

CHAPTER 48

A Brief Encounter with Royalty

The wedding of Prince Edward and Sophie Rhys-Jones took place on 19th June 1999 in St George's Chapel at Windsor Castle. Prince Edward announced his engagement to Sophie Rhys-Jones on 6th January 1999, so, for such a major State occasion, time was short to make all the arrangements. Our task (as The Royal Band) for the wedding was to provide a 14-piece fanfare team and brass group to play from the organ loft of the Chapel throughout the service, and thereafter supply the Dance Band for the reception in St George's Hall Windsor Castle. These plans began to take shape over the winter months and it was late April by the time meetings were arranged at Windsor Castle to fine tune details.

As it happened I was in Bangkok Thailand with the band for the St George's Day celebrations on 23rd April, an annual event arranged by the St George's Day Society (a popular 10-day trip on which Cay could accompany me). It was on the long flight back to the UK that I received a message that Prince Edward and Sophie Rhys-Jones would like me to join them for a meeting in Windsor Castle shortly after landing at Heathrow Airport. The Band Secretary fixed a car to pick me up at the airport and take me to the meeting, which was as far removed from the experiences of Bangkok as it was possible to imagine! I met the Royal couple and the organist in a small room in The Castle. We discussed the music for the ceremony and the music for the reception afterwards. In truth the wedding ceremony was relatively easy from a music point of view and the organist was already on top of the content. The Royal couple were charming as ever and it was an honour to be part of their detailed planning. I had always liked Prince Edward and had seen him many times in his early childhood in Britannia for the Western Isles trips.

There was a very real connection between the Portsmouth Band and the Royal Family forged over the many years service in HMY Britannia, so it was quite an honour for us to be the main music group for the whole of the reception. The dance band, led by George Tate, did themselves proud with their performance, the highlight of which was a 'Blues Brothers' tribute, always a great favourite with the Royals. After it was all done and dusted, I had a very nice note *(see Appendix 3)* from the happy couple thanking us for our input. This was to be the last major Royal event that I was to be involved with. I had played a musical part in all the Royal Weddings from Prince Charles to Prince Edward and I suppose not many musicians can say that!

A Christmas Festival

The Band of HM Royal Marines Portsmouth (Royal Band)
The Chichester Cathedral Choir, organist and Choir Master: Alan Thurlow BA FRCO
The St Richard Singers
Director of Music: Major John Perkins ARAM MMus ARCM LGSM RM
Producer: Bob Whitney, Engineer: Tony Faulkner. Editor: Bob Whitney
Recorded in Chichester Cathedral 19th and 20th October 1999

Strong links had been forged between The Band of HM Royal Marines Portsmouth and the Chichester Cathedral Choir over the years as the two organisations shared the platform each Christmas for the seasonal festival of music in The Chichester Theatre. We already knew each other well and there existed a catalogue of repertoire that we had built up over the years. This presented another opportunity.

Cat. No: CLCD11799

The wonderful setting and acoustic of the Cathedral was beautifully captured by the special skills of Tony Faulkner and Bob Whitney from Clovelly Recordings, and we were fortunate to be joined by The St Richard Singers who added greatly to the rousing arrangements of carols. The 24bit recording was made using state-of-the-art dCS technology over the 19th and 20th October 1999 in a chilly Cathedral and was great fun from start to finish. Definitely worth a listen in early December to get you in the Christmas spirit! This was a fun project.

Ron and Don's Millennium Cruise

In early 2000 a little gem of a cruise around the Mediterranean came from nowhere and was to prove one of the most remarkable short trips[61] of my career - and there were many over the years. Sir Donald Gosling (RIP) and his business partner Sir Ronald Hobson (RIP) were the owners of National Car Parks (NCP), the London based business that bought up brown field sites in city centres to provide cheap parking.

By the mid-1990s NCP had become one of the most successful private businesses in Britain. In 1998 the company was bought by US-based property and travel services provider Cendant for £801million with Hobson, Gosling, and their family trusts who owned 72.5% of the National Parking Corporation receiving £580million.

---

[61] There were many such one-off trips down the years, the like of which is seldom found in the civilian music world. The confidence in booking a military band carries with it all sorts of guarantees of quality and behaviour that is invaluable to sponsors.

By the millennium Ron and Don had been in business together for over 50 years and become two of the wealthiest men in Britain. To celebrate this happy circumstance they decided to host a millennium cruise around the Mediterranean.

The cruise was to be on the 6-star Norwegian cruiser The Seabourn Spirit[62] and to include around 180 guests (including me, Cay and 14 musicians from the Portsmouth Band) who would be showered with gifts and hospitality of the highest and most extravagant type for twelve days. The whole trip was funded entirely by Ron and Don including

Cay and I trying to understand the Lifeboat Drills!

chartering a Jumbo Jet from Heathrow to Venice and back for our happy band of guests. Other guests included a selection of senior military figures both serving and retired, including Sea Lords and a former Commandant General Royal Marines - Sir Don was fiercely proud of being an honorary Royal Naval Commodore. All manner of broadcasters and entertainers such as Ned Sherrin[63], Dickie Davies, Ronnie Corbett, Tim Rice, Terry Wogan, Robert Powell (and Babs) and a large array of sporting and TV personality types made up our number. This included the ventriloquist Roger De Courcey and Nookie Bear who it transpired was a distant relation of Cay's (Roger, not Nookie Bear!!). These were our travelling companions for the duration; a little like 'Death on the Nile' on steroids, without the death!

Our role was to provide the occasional entertainment throughout the day by way of background music with jazz combinations, two open-air concerts on the sun deck and to accompany artists such as Terry Wogan, Ronnie Corbett and others during the after dinner impromptu 'sods opera' on a couple of evenings. A piece of cake as they say. Everyone was very relaxed and easy to get along with and we had a wonderful trip around the Med seeing how billionaires live. We even had breakfast on the deck alongside an erupting Mount Etna, the famous volcano located on the East coast of the Italian island of Sicily, in the Mediterranean. What a spectacular start to the day! This was a case in point to prove the worth of service musicians who were able to quickly adapt to the lavish situation and provide a range of musical combinations at the drop of a hat,

62 The Seabourn Spirit is a small ship fitted for 200 passengers and 140 crew.

63 The producer, director, writer, satirist and raconteur, Ned Sherrin broadcast live an edition of 'Loose Ends' from the cruise.

without abusing the free bar too much! A memorable trip in my last few months in the Band Service.

This wonderful twelve-day trip was to be my last engagement with the Portsmouth Band of any consequence. My final weeks were filled with writing reports on the 80 plus people on my books and saying au revoir to friends in the Portsmouth area. I had decided to take six months completely off and work on my violin playing to see whether I could make a living as a full-time player. I would not look for employment until the following summer once I had cleared my mind and felt ready to start again. As it transpired I never did take an employed job for the next 20 years because freelance playing, conducting, writing, recording (mostly producing), charity work for both the RNLI and the Deal Memorial Bandstand, property development, travel....... and so on! A different, yet equally fulfilling second career grew from nowhere, resulting from my own initiative, minimal administration, maximum music, my own boss - perfect, but another story!

John leaving The Portsmouth Band - November 2000
Presentation by WO1 Bandmaster Steve Savage

CHAPTER 49

On the Home Front

Cay and I had always tried to move together as different appointments came along, the only exception was my two years as Director of Music at the Commando Training Centre in Devon 1992/94. The decision for Cay to stay in Deal for this period was largely due to the fact that my first six months with the Commandos Band was either touring the Far East on the Aircraft Carrier HMS Invincible or on the Initial Staff Officers Course in RNC Greenwich, a three-month course spent designing warships, helicopters, writing service papers, Naval strategy and procurement.

As a family we had liked the West Country on our previous appointment in HMS Raleigh, Torpoint, Cornwall between 1984/88, so it was a not a hard decision for us (Nick and Steve were still at boarding school in West Sussex) to return to Torpoint once again. I had been promoted to Captain in 1994 to take up the appointment as Director of Music Plymouth, which was now a large size Staff Band numbering twice as many musicians and buglers as my previous band at the Commando Training Centre. It was fairly clear to me that there was little or no chance of me becoming the Principal Director of Music[64] as the incumbent was only one year older than me and it was customary for Lieutenant Colonels to be offered a two-year extension. That would of course rule me out (and so it proved a few years later) and therefore I

On holiday with family in New York
2017 - US Open Tennis Flushing Meadows - less grandson Pablo

---

[64] My only realistic chance of the PDM job was if David Cole (who was old enough to give me a chance) was promoted PDM before me. Then maybe Phil Watson after me would have worked well.

saw no reason why I couldn't finish off my last five years with the Plymouth Band. Historically five years was not an exceptional length of time for Directors to stay with a Staff Band. I applied through the normal channels to do just this and was informed that I had to be moved to Portsmouth to take over as Director of Music Training in the spring of 1996, a job considered a pre-requisite of PDM!

We eventually found rented accommodation in Waterlooville just outside of Portsmouth. It was a nice detached house on the A3 main road leading towards Portsmouth and we rented the house through the Naval 'Hiring' scheme. We quickly settled into our new situation which is just as well as my new job was a full-on challenge. Quite apart from having to achieve degree accreditation for Royal Marines Music Training as outlined earlier, The Armed Forces Music Bursary Scheme needed to be resolved and we had to find ways to make the RMSM function effectively in the new buildings we inherited.

We spent about 18 months in Waterlooville before moving to a Married Quarter in Pembroke Park, Old Portsmouth. The house was a walk away from my place of work, so much easier than commuting from Waterlooville in the long traffic queues. We all liked Old Portsmouth and the Southsea seafront, and it was very convenient for Nick and Steve who took their first degrees at Southampton University. We stayed in Old Portsmouth until March 2000 when Cay moved back to Deal and I moved into the Wardroom Mess of HMS Nelson.

In the Spring of 1997 we had visited our longtime friends John and Jane Cullis in Deal for the weekend. John and Jane live on Deal Seafront towards the North end of the town - a terrific spot. Directly behind their house was a large disused garage that had been in earlier times small industrial units and originally an old sardine canning factory. John and Jane had acquired this derelict plot and had engaged developers to convert the site into four dwellings and to build four further town houses on the seafront side of the plot. At the time of our visit the work was in the early stages of redevelopment, but the potential was clear to see. Before travelling back to Portsmouth on the Sunday we had a guided tour of the work so far and were very impressed with the scale of the project, the size and space available and the quality of the design and build. By 4pm the same day we had pulled the car over on the A3 and made an offer for No 1 The Old Cannery, where we live today, 23 years later!

By the time I moved into the Wardroom Mess in April 2000 I started to understand what 'the beginning of the end' felt like. Apart from one or two musical engagements to plan for in the early Spring, there was little on the horizon for me to look forward to professionally. The summer was dominated with Massed Bands or outdoor events which held little attraction for me and after summer leave I would have about six weeks to kill in Portsmouth before my terminal leave leading towards my retirement date of 28th November 2000. By June I realised that I was just 'marking time' waiting for the date to come around, not enjoying being separated from my family who were in Deal, bored with living in the Mess and, with little meaningful work to do, I felt it was time for me to go. I applied to leave a few months early and to my surprise was given a few months 'gardening' leave in order that it didn't affect my full pension - very generous - thanks. So in July 2000 I left Portsmouth and the life I had known for a little over 35 years for what was to become a whole new adventure. I was ready for it.

Odds and Ends

Always watch the conductor?

My obsession with memorable concerts for the wrong reasons was given a boost in 1999. Towards the end of my time in Portsmouth I played in a concert in Portsmouth for an old friend who was

John's final visit to Britannia in Leith Scotland - August 2000

conductor of a large community orchestra in the city. The programme of music included The Symphony No. 2 in E minor, Op. 27 by Rachmaninoff, which was chosen to stretch the abilities of the players. I was sat on the outside of the second desk of first violins which is very close to the conductor, maybe eight feet or so. My desk partner was another old friend Lesley who I bumped into recently which brought back this memory.

This fabulous symphony had been well rehearsed and the performance was going well. The first violin part is very technical, particularly the final movement which becomes ever higher, faster and louder, culminating in the last page of the piece which requires total concentration. Our very able conductor, who was doing a great job, became over excited and threw himself to one side with a most extravagant gesture, causing him to slip off the small conductor's podium and fall to the ground with a crash. He was clearly dazed. All this was happening within eight feet of me and Lesley. Maestro shook himself, stood up and continued conducting with the same vigour that had caused his downfall. Unfortunately, in his haste, he was facing and conducting the audience! After a few priceless moments he gathered his composure, turned around and finished the last few bars of the symphony in triumph!

I had been watching this whole process, the like of which I had never seen before, with incredulity. When the music finished and the rapturous applause (due in no small part to the conductor's recovery) started, I turned to Lesley and said, "Wow, did you see that?". Lesley replied, "See what?" She, and the majority of the orchestra, didn't see any of this!

Always watch the conductor?

CHAPTER 50

Reflections

Looking back, my service career was almost a textbook success, rising through every rank to become a commissioned officer and retiring at the rank of Major as Director of Music of 'The Royal Band'. I was happy and grateful for the good fortune that had come my way. However, I was left feeling that it rather fizzled out and I finished on a decrescendo rather than a crescendo!

In a musical career spanning well over 50 years I realise how lucky I have been. The single most fortunate thing that happened to me was to join The Royal Marines Band Service, which gave me a top-class music education and a range of personal and leadership skills that have served me well down the years. I have met so many wonderful people and enjoyed countless privileged insights into the Royal Family and other high-profile leaders and entertainers. It was the norm.

In later years I have managed to continue with the music I love the most, chamber music, and make a living as a violinist, conductor and record producer. I have had considerable success as an arranger and composer and my arrangement and recording of 'The Ashokan Farewell' has remained in the Classic FM Hall of Fame top 60 for 24 years and counting - being voted No 3 in the chart in 2003. The recording is by far the highest selling military recording of all time. I have played in most all of the top concert halls in the UK and many of the leading venues around the world, a retirement highlight appearing as violin soloist with The Royal Philharmonic Orchestra in June 2001 in a live broadcast (for Classic FM) from London's Royal Albert Hall.

I have travelled to all parts of the world (more than once in many cases) and taken part in International events on a regular basis. I am fortunate now to be able to travel much of the year, spending a large amount of time in the USA, France and Spain, as well as England. When in the UK our home remains in Deal where it all started.

Our most important achievement is our family of which we are so proud. Nick and Miranda live in Manhattan New York and have three children, Jack aged 12, Cole aged 9 and Annabel aged 7 (going on 15!). We visit New York every year at least once or as much as three times depending on our energy levels and funds! Steve and Kat live in Haywards Heath with their son Pablo aged 23 who has just graduated from Durham University with a Physics degree. We see lots of them as they are less than two hours drive from Deal.

I have always been someone who is looking forward to the next thing and have rarely reminisced about the past, but it has been fun looking back over my early life in The Royal Marines for the first time and remembering both the good and less good times. I am sure all lives have their ups and downs and mine could be the story of many of my contemporaries who were fortunate to live at a time when there were no World Wars, unlike our parents' generation, and an abundance of opportunities for those willing to take them. They say 'timing is everything', so how lucky were we? The last twenty years since retiring from the Royal Marines have been almost as eventful as my military career, possibly even more diverse, but that is another story.

My retirement bash held in Deal November 2000
Many of the old team from Britannia days (pictured above)
made the journey down to join me.

CHAPTER 51

Regrets

I've had a few. I wished I had started learning the violin earlier in life, certainly before I was 15 years of age. Crucial early years were lost to me and, although I was a quick learner and had natural aptitude, I was always at a disadvantage at the highest levels of playing in comparison to those who started as a child.

I wish I had learned the art of pizzicato!

I wish I had been less quick to voice my opinions, especially when something negative needed to be said! I was generally the one who put my proverbial 'head above the parapet' when others said nothing and let things slide. It did the others no harm but it cost me from time to time. Nobody remembers these heroic efforts to call out injustices.

I wish I had been more patient generally.

I often wished I had specialised more. Maybe the violin, composition or conducting - or golf! The nature of the DOM job meant I spent far too much time in routine administrative work, at one time well over four years without any music whatsoever!

I have mixed feelings about our decision to send the boys to boarding school. It was made for the right reasons as we were always on the move, but we were never happy dropping them off on a Sunday evening or not being able to get to pick them up for the weekend. However, the confidence, sense of adventure and independence they have is all connected in my view.

I wish we had attended the Decommissioning Ceremony of Britannia on 11 December 1997 to which we were invited. I guess I was still too angry at the loss. Cay has yet to forgive me!

I wish I had been more of a 'team' player at work. I was too easily frustrated by the lack of vision and indifference I saw in some others. I was always more effective when I was in sole charge by myself away from negative vibes. My enthusiasm sometimes resulted in my bosses seeing me as a competitor. I learned the hard way that bosses like to see you doing well, but not too well!

I wish I could turn the clocks back and do it all again!

Appendix One

HMY Britannia - Facts and Figures

A beautiful original watercolour of Britannia alongside in Portsmouth Dockyard
Presented to me by Ken and Karen Peers on my retirement from the RMs in November 2000
Painted by C L Roberts

Background

The Royal Yacht Britannia served the British Royal Family for over 44 years. This famous ship was the last in a line of 83 Royal Yachts, a tradition that began in the 1660s. Britannia travelled over one million nautical miles on 968 State visits. She was a successful ambassador around the world and played a key role in major historic events. It was decided that Britannia should be commissioned and double as a hospital ship in time of war. It was also hoped a convalescence cruise would help King George VI ailing health. The John Brown shipyard in Clydebank received the order from the Admiralty for a new ship on 4 February, 1952. Sadly King George VI, The Queen's father, passed away two days later. Not only did The Queen now have to prepare for her new role, but she also had responsibility for the commissioning of the new Royal Yacht.

Britannia has five decks that include State Apartments, the State Dining Room and Drawing Room and even a garage which houses one of The Queen's Rolls-Royce. Britannia's royal apartments were designed by Sir Hugh Casson and are distinguished by their modest elegance. Britannia was not meant to be opulent but offers instead country-house comfort. The Queen's and the Duke of Edinburgh's bedrooms are relatively plain. The Royal Yacht Britannia was fitted in such a way that it could be transformed into a hospital in time of war. The facilities included an operating table, a sick bay and a dentist's chair.

Built in Scotland

John Brown & Co was one of the most famous shipyards in the world, having built the famous liners Queen Elizabeth and Queen Mary. The keel of the new Royal Yacht was laid down in June 1952. One of the last fully-riveted ships to be built with a remarkably smooth painted hull, she was finally ready to be launched on 16 April 1953. The ship's name was a closely guarded secret, only being revealed when the Queen smashed a bottle of Empire wine and announced "I name this ship Britannia… I wish success to her and all who sail in her". After the launch, Britannia's building work continued as her funnel and masts were installed, before beginning sea trials on 3 November 1953 off the West Coast of Scotland. On successful completion, she was commissioned into the Royal Navy on 11 January 1954.

Facts and Figures

Laid down: June 1952 at John Brown & Co. Ltd, Clydebank
Designer / Builder: Sir Victor Shepheard, Director of Naval Construction; and John Brown & Co. Ltd
Launched: 16 April 1953 by HM Queen Elizabeth II
Commissioned: At sea, 11 January 1954
Length overall: 125.65m or 412ft 3in (ferry 700ft)
Length on waterline: 115.82m or 380ft
Load displacement: 4715 tons
Gross tonnage: 5862 tons
Speed: 22.5 knots maximum 21 knots continuous
Engines: Two geared steam turbines, developing a total of 12,000 shaft horse power. Two main boilers, and an auxiliary boiler for harbour requirements by Foster Wheeler
Range: 2,196 miles at 20 knots (burning diesel fuel)
2,553 miles at 18 knots (burning diesel fuel)
Main Mast Height: 42.44m or 139ft 3in - Royal Standard
Fore Mast Height: 40.54m or 133ft - Lord Admiral's Flag
Mizzen Mast Height: 36.22m or 118ft 10in - Union Flag
Fuel & water: 330 tons of fuel oil providing a range of 2,000 miles at 20 knots. 120 tons of fresh water. Additional tanks can increase fuel capacity to 490 tons and fresh water capacity to 195 tons

Maiden Voyage

Britannia sailed on her maiden voyage from Portsmouth to Grand Harbour, Malta, departing on 14 April and arriving on 22 April 1954. She carried Princess Anne and Prince Charles to Malta in order for them to meet the Queen and Prince Philip in Tobruk at the end of the royal couple's Commonwealth Tour. The Queen and Prince Philip embarked on Britannia for the first time in Tobruk on 1 May 1954.

The crew of Royal Yachtsmen were volunteers from the general service of the Royal Navy. Officers were appointed for up to two years, while the 'yachtsmen' were drafted as volunteers and after 365 days' service could be admitted to 'The Permanent Royal Yacht Service' as Royal Yachtsmen and served until they chose to leave the Royal Yacht Service or were dismissed for medical or disciplinary reasons. As a result, some served in Britannia for 25 years or more. The ship also carried a detachment of 8 Royal Marines and a Royal Marines Band of 26 musicians and buglers.

Discipline was managed by a series of warnings or being dismissed Royal Yacht and flown home to rejoin general service with the Fleet.

When the Royals arrived aboard everything changed to Royal Duties routines and Britannia reverted to a Royal Palace where the ship's company broadly lived and worked forward of midships and the Royal Family worked and lived aft of midships. There was lots of crossover and the Royals would regularly pop into messes around the ship and take part in many of the lighter activities which are part of life at sea.

During her career as Royal Yacht, Britannia conveyed the Queen, other members of the Royal Family and various dignitaries on 696 foreign visits and 272 visits in British waters. In this time, Britannia steamed 1,087,623 nautical miles (2,014,278 km).

Uses and Costs

In addition to her official duties Britannia provided the Royal Family with a place to relax, in particular the Royal Family's annual cruise of the Western Isles, and was also increasingly used with considerable success to promote British industry abroad. It has also been used for entertaining and receptions as well as for honeymoon tours (Princess Margaret 1960, Princess Anne's 1973, Prince Charles and Lady Diana 1981). It has been estimated that while in Commission, the Royal Yacht Britannia cost the public £7K per week when in service and £4K when stationary, not including fuel costs. Famous guests included Dwight Eisenhower, Gerald Ford and Ronald Reagan, Winston Churchill, Nelson Mandela and Boris Yeltsin.

Decommissioning

In 1997, the Conservative government committed itself to replacing the Royal Yacht if re-elected, while the Labour Party refused to disclose its plans for the vessel. After Labour won the general election in May 1997, it announced the vessel was to be retired and no replacement would be built (and with it went my next job as Director of Music of the Royal Yacht Band!).

The previous government had argued that the cost was justified by its role in foreign policy and promoting British interests abroad, particularly through conferences held by British Invisibles, formerly the Committee on Invisible Exports. It was estimated by the Overseas Trade Board that events held on board the yacht helped raise £3 billion for the treasury between 1991 and 1995 alone. The new government said the expenditure could not be justified given other pressures on the defence budget, from which a replacement vessel would have been funded and maintained.

The Royal Yacht's last foreign mission was to convey the last governor of Hong Kong, Chris Patten (now Lord Patten of Barnes), and the Prince of Wales back from Hong Kong after its handover to the People's Republic of China on 1 July 1997. Britannia was decommissioned on 11 December 1997. The Queen is reported to have shed a tear at the decommissioning ceremony that was attended by most of the senior members of the Royal Family. When Britannia was decommissioned in 1997, it marked the end of a long tradition of British Royal Yachts, dating back to 1660 and the reign of Charles II. In total, the British Monarchy has had 83 Royal Yachts. Britannia was the first Royal Yacht to be built with complete ocean-going capacity and designed as a royal residence to entertain guests around the world. Previously Royal Navy warships or passenger liners were commandeered for overseas Royal tours. Listed as part of the National Historic Fleet, Britannia is a visitor attraction moored in the Port of Leith in Edinburgh, Scotland, and is cared for by the Royal Yacht Britannia Trust, a registered charity. There was some controversy over the siting of the ship, with some arguing that she would be better moored on the River Clyde, where she was built, rather than in Edinburgh, with which the yacht had few links. However, her positioning in Leith coincided with a redevelopment of the harbour area, and the advent of Scottish devolution.

Odds and Ends

Practical considerations included a garage for the Queen's Rolls-Royce, a mahogany windbreak on the bridge to prevent gusts from lifting skirts, and a knighting stool to be carried on all voyages. On April 16, 1953, the Queen launched her from Clydeside and she would complete more than a million miles over her 44 years of service. The Queen described the ship as 'the one place where I can truly relax'. To this day the clocks on board remain at 3.01pm, the time the Queen stepped off for the last time.

Appendix Two

Royal National Lifeboat Institution and Music

Brian Williams has been an RNLI member now for well over 70 years. It all started when serving at the Royal Marines Barracks in Deal, Kent when he became part of the launching crew for the Walmer lifeboat. Brian joined the Royal Marines under the Admiralty 'Youth' Scheme, which meant 4 months at Oxford University (Brasenose College) then Deal – OTU Thurlestone – Commissioned Royal Marines Officer - Commando Training at Achnacarry and Towyn. Over the years he has supported the lifeboat service in many ways and in a number of branches. As a miniature model specialist he has completed countless lifeboat replicas for lifeboat crew-members and there is nearly always a lifeboat model under construction in his tiny 'shipyard'. He completed a whole collection of miniature models of lifeboats for RNLI headquarters for use in the RNLI Museum and for fund-raising.

In 1986 he formed the Rame Peninsula Branch RNLI and, in 1992 as its Chairman, was responsible for commissioning the first official RNLI march from the Royal Marines Band Service, 'The Lifeboatmen' composed by Musician Trevor Brown. The march was recorded by Lieutenant John Perkins and the Band of HM Royal Marines Commandos in 1993 on the album 'Marches of the Sea' and was an immediate success and source of fund-raising for the RNLI. A sequel recording made in 1994 by Captain John Perkins and The Band of HM Royal Marines Plymouth as a tribute to the RNLI, 'For Those in Peril on the Sea', made clear that there was a need for a more formal marketing arrangement to be put in place to manage the projects. HQ RNLI had no experience in marketing recordings so in 1993 Brian Williams was asked to undertake this role.

To conform to the Charities Act, Brian handed over the Rame RNLI Branch to others and formed the RNLI West Country Group, setting up a mail order business to sell the recordings. Other recordings were developed and added to the list. The West Country Marketing Group was appointed Distributor for all Royal Marines band recordings and was appointed the RNLI Music Division in 1996, directly responsible to the Managing Director of RNLI (Sales) Ltd at Poole. There are over thirty recordings for which Brian has been responsible, not only those of the Royal Marines but others developed by the RNLI Music Division. The uncompromising standards of the Royal Marines and Clovelly Recordings Ltd (with whom the warmest collaboration resulted) ensured the recordings met the exacting standards of the lifeboat service, and an enormous financial success resulted. From 1993 to 2006, over 40,000 copies were sold and nearly £300,000 raised for lifeboat funds.

In 2005 the RNLI Music Division Chairman, Brian Williams, received the highest award that can be bestowed on an RNLI volunteer by being elected by the Council of the RNLI to be an

Honorary Life Governor. In 2009 Brian was honoured by being made an MBE in recognition of his work for the RNLI over many years.

In 2006 Clovelly Recordings, Ltd was honoured to receive the RNLI's 'Retailer of the Year Award' for their enormous support and contribution to the lifeboat service.

Brian H Williams MBE

Major John Perkins, me and the RNLI

"I first became acquainted with John in the mid 1980s when I was regularly in touch with him and the then Band of HM Royal Marines Flag Officer Plymouth at HMS Raleigh. We instantly hit it off as friends. Knowing of my support of the RNLI an idea gelled between us of the possibility of adding to RNLI funds by creating recordings by the band and their subsequent sales.

To fund this I successfully sought sponsorship by a group of West Country companies to sponsor the costs in carrying out the recording at EMI's Abbey Road Studios. 'Marches of the Sea' was recorded by John and The Band of HM Royal Marines Commandos in June 1993. The following year when John was DOM of The Band of HM Royal Marines Plymouth, the second recording, 'For Those in Peril on the Sea', was also completed at Abbey Road sponsored by the RNLI West Country Group.

Then 25 years ago in 1995 'The Ashokan Farewell' was arranged by John for solo violin and concert band for a tour of the United States of America by The Plymouth band. I have never forgotten the spellbinding effect on the Torpoint audience when John played this new arrangement for the very first time in the UK in the Roebuck Theatre. 'The Ashokan Farewell' became the title track of an album of virtuoso solos recorded by John and the Plymouth Band at Abbey Road Studios, with my help in getting sponsorship once again! The recording went straight to No 36 in the Classic Hall of Fame and every year since has never been lower than No 52 being voted as high as No 3 in 2003. It is a truly remarkable achievement by any standards.

A number of highly successful recordings with John and his bands followed over the next few years leaving a legacy of recordings, second to none.

I cannot over emphasise the warmth of the relationship between me, and my wife Pat, with John and Cay over the years we worked together. As we used to say – whatever problems arose, everything always worked out, and we had fun!"

Brian H Williams MBE

189

Appendix Two (cont.)

RNLI Award 2006

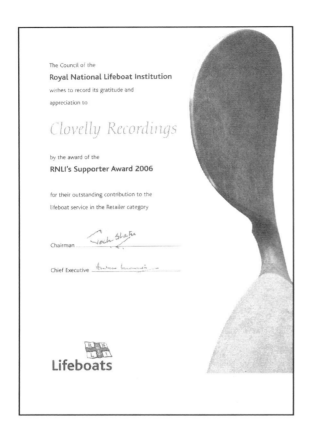

John receiving the
RNLI's Supporter Award 2006
From Princess Alexandra in
London's Barbican Theatre

A treasured memento from the
RNLI reflecting the part Clovelly
Recordings Ltd played in raising
almost £300K for RNLI funds

Appendix Three

Royal Wedding thanks

Saturday 19th June 1999
St George's Chapel Windsor

BUCKINGHAM PALACE

22 December 1999

Dear Captain Perkins,

Please forgive us for not writing sooner to thank you and the band for helping to make our wedding so very special. It may seem as if it all happened ages ago, but it is still vivid for us, as is the enormous effort so many people like yourself made to ensure it all worked beautifully.

The music was fantastic, and that's not just our opinion. So many people have commented on the superb quality of the music, most especially the dance band – another triumph! Several have been amazed, as always, that the fanfare team, the extra instruments in the Chapel and the dance band were all the same musicians.

Would you please pass on our sincerest thanks to everyone whom we know worked very hard to get everything perfect. We hope you will accept this small memento as a token of our appreciation. We're just sorry it has taken so long to get it to you!

Yours sincerely,

Sophie + Edward

Captain J R Perkins, RM

Appendix Four

Commandant General's Commendation - July 2018

COMMANDANT GENERAL ROYAL MARINES COMMENDATION
MAJOR JOHN PERKINS ROYAL MARINES (RTD)

John Perkins joined the Royal Marines School of Music, Deal, in 1965 at the age of fourteen. His ability and potential were noted early in his career with the award of the Commandant General's Certificate for the most promising student. He became the first Warrant Officer Class 1 Bandmaster to be commissioned, after which he served in a variety of appointments as a Director of Music until his retirement in 2000. A prolific composer and arranger, he has produced many recordings throughout his career including the renowned *Ashokan Farewell*, in which he featured as solo violinist, a firm 'Classic FM Hall of Fame' favourite.

John is currently the Chairman of the Deal Memorial Bandstand Trust which is dedicated to preserving the Memorial Bandstand; it is a 'living' and fitting memorial to the eleven Royal Marines musicians who were killed by the IRA on 22 September 1989 and bears the names of those who were lost. The Memorial Bandstand is a focal point for the people of Deal and is the venue for a series of concerts throughout the Summer months the high point of which is the annual Rededication Service by the band of her Majesty's Royal Marines, to which the families of the eleven are invited. This major annual event regularly attracts audiences in excess of 10,000 people and since the closure of the Deal Barracks, continues to nurture the longstanding relationship between the people of Deal and the Royal Marines.

After twelve years of outstanding leadership as the Chairman of the Deal Memorial Bandstand Trust, John is retiring once again. Through his leadership and innovation, he has improved the governance of the Trust and assured the long-term financial viability of the Memorial Bandstand, identifying sponsors to meet the day-to-day operational costs and securing additional funding for capital expenditure projects to maintain and improve the structure and facilities.

On his retirement, John's leadership and effective stewardship will leave the Deal Memorial Bandstand in a strong financial position and with a clear sense of purpose for the future. For his many years of commitment to the Royal Marines, both while serving in the Royal Marines Band Service and latterly as the Chairman of the Deal Memorial Bandstand Trust, John Perkins is awarded a Commandant General Royal Marines Commendation.

C R Stickland OBE
Major General
Commandant General Royal Marines

15 July 2018

CGRM's Commendation presented to John on 15th July 2018 for
12 years as Chairman of the Deal Memorial Bandstand Trust

Appendix Five

Life after Royal Marines

The Perkins Boys
L to R: Pablo, John, Nick, Steve

Chamber Music
L to R: Martin Thomas, Steve Shakeshaft, John
Perkins, John Georgiadis

Conductor: The Kent Concert Orchestra

Chairman - The Deal Memorial Bandstand

Countless hours producing recordings

Regular violin soloist. Playing the Bach
Double Violin Concerto with John Georgiadis,
former Leader of the LSO

Printed in Great Britain
by Amazon